Another Nice Mess

The Laurel & Hardy Story

Donated by
the author
December 2011

by

Raymond Valinoti, Jr.

Published in the USA by:
BearManor Media
P O Box 71426
Albany, Georgia 31708
www.bearmanormedia.com

Printed in the United States of America
ISBN 978-1-59393-546-7

Book and cover design and layout by Darlene Swanson • www.van-garde.com

Contents

Introduction

It was September 15, 1926. The location was Hal Roach Studios in Hollywood, California. Stan Laurel, a delicately handsome auburn-haired Englishman, was pleased with himself. He had just completed a screenplay based on a theatre sketch his father wrote back in 1905 called *Home from the Honeymoon*. The scenario was about two hoboes on the lam who take refuge in a vacant mansion. When a well-to-do couple drops by, the tramps masquerade as the owner and the maid. (Yes, one of the men dresses as a woman!) Their charade backfires when the real owner returns unexpectedly.

As a professional comedian, Mr. Laurel cast himself as one of the bums. His character was a good-natured dimwit who clumsily tried to carry out his partner's orders. The other hobo would be the domineering partner, acting as though he knew everything but just as inept. Who would play this role?

There is no record who made the decision and why, but Oliver Hardy, a portly, cherubic faced American actor known to his friends as "Babe," was chosen. Mr. Hardy had appeared with Mr. Laurel in two earlier films, *The Lucky Dog* and *45 Minutes from Hollywood*. But for this film, Babe would be Stan's teammate for the first time. Filming took place in late September. It was released on March 13, 1927 under the title *Duck Soup*.

And thus a legendary comedy duo was born, a duo that would bring joy and laughter to millions throughout the world. Not that anyone at Hal Roach Studios knew this at the time. Indeed, Stan and Babe would appear in a few subsequent pictures not as a team, but as two individual actors who happened to appear on the same screen. Gradually people realized that whenever they shared a scene, a marvelous chemistry sparkled between them. Individually they were very good but together, they were sensational. And so Hal Roach Studios officially marketed Laurel and Hardy as a team and they immediately won the public's hearts.

At that time, Stan Laurel was thirty-seven years old and Oliver Hardy was thirty-five. They had both performed in films for many years. How did they wind up together at Hal Roach Studios? To answer this question, we should explore each of their lives before they teamed up.

An Aspiring Comedian From Lancashire

Stan Laurel was born Arthur Stanley Jefferson in Ulverston, Lancashire, England on June 16, 1890. Ulverston is a town in northwestern England in Great Britain. It hasn't changed much in over a century since Stan's birth. Some of the streets are still cobbled, the same adjacent houses from a century ago are still around, their exteriors look just as they did in the late nineteenth century, and an old clock tower that was the town's landmark during Stan's childhood still stands.

Back then, Queen Victoria reigned over an empire that spread all over the world. Britain was a rich and powerful nation blessed with thriving industries that ensured its prosperity. Among these was the theatrical industry. In the late nineteenth century, radio and television did not exist and movies were experimental novelties that were too primitive for the public. So the average Britisher went to the theater for amusement.

Stan's parents thrived in the theatre business. His father, Arthur Jefferson, acted, wrote plays, and managed various theatres in England and Scotland with great energy. An auburn-haired gentleman with imposing features, he strove to look the part of the prosperous theatrical producer, elegantly dressed in custom tailored suits and ties.

Arthur was also determined to present his theatrical productions to everyone regardless of social standing. Not all Britishers benefited from the country's prosperity. Those who could not support themselves were forced into poorhouses where they had to do menial labor for food and shelter. Arthur would arrange special matinees for the inmates there, giving packages of tea, sugar, and tobacco to the adults and shoes and stockings to the children.

Stan's mother, Margaret Jefferson, a pretty brunette, was an actress. She performed under the name Madge Metcalfe in several of her husband's productions. Madge also helped decorate his theatres and design his stage sets. She had a beautiful singing voice. As an adult, Stan recalled her singing a traditional Scottish song, "Annie Laurie" to him when he was very little.

Stan was the second oldest of five children. He had one sister and three brothers; one of the brothers died in infancy. Because Arthur managed theatres in England and Scotland and Madge acted in his plays, the Jeffersons were often on the road. All the children came along, except Stan who was a sickly baby. He stayed at home with his grandparents, George and Sarah Metcalfe, in Ulverston.

The Metcalfes showered Stan with love and affection but they were stern disciplinarians. If Stan misbehaved, George banished him to a dark wash house, used for cleaning clothes, in the back yard. The boy would have to sit there until he had learned his lesson. Being a mischievous child, Stan frequently visited the wash house but he didn't mind it. He stashed away comics, matches, and candles there so he could read by candlelight.

When Grandma Metcalfe went shopping, she would take young Stan along, and sometimes buy him treacle toffee, a popular sweet in Britain. He loved to dawdle and look into the shops' big plate glass windows. Grandma Metcalfe often would lose Stan and have to retrace her footsteps. She would frequently find him peering through the glass and making faces at his reflection.

When Stan was about six, the Jeffersons moved from Ulverston to North Shields in northeastern England because this town was closer to Arthur's theatres. Stan was enrolled in a boarding school in Bishop Auckland, another northeastern town. When the boy was home on weekends, Arthur let him hang around backstage at the Theatre Royal in North Shields. One can imagine Stan's excitement watching the performers enact larger than life characterizations in imaginative dramas as they created fanciful worlds. What a beguiling experience, he must have thought, to be on the stage! He began spending his pocket money on toy theatres, Punch and Judy shows, marionettes, shadowgraphs (photographic images resembling shadows), magic lanterns- anything related to the theatre.

Stan became so interested in show business that when he was nine, his father's theatre staff helped him convert their home's attic into a miniature theatre, able to seat twenty to thirty people. There was an admission fee but those without cash could get in if they contributed any stage props- rugs, curtains, crockery, and household articles. Along with other children, Stan created the "Stanley Jefferson Amateur Dramatic Society," proclaiming himself its Director, Manager, Author, Producer, and Leading Man.

For their first intended presentation, Stan wrote a play based on one of his father's melodramas. The play's program promised,

"Excitement! Struggles! And *murders!*" As the dashing hero, Stan would pursue a bloodthirsty villain and bring him to justice in a climactic battle. Stan cast a butcher's son named Harold, whose admission fee was two white mice, as the scoundrel. Stan thought Harold's bulldog like features not only made him suitably hateful, but that they would generate audience sympathy for the hero.

The dramatic struggle on the night of the performance enthralled the audience, the parents cheering their children and the girls cheering whichever boys they fancied. As the culminating battle took place, cries like "Stick it, Stan!" and "Good lad, Harold!" rang throughout the makeshift theater. The boys hurled any available objects at each other and then took off their outer garments to eagerly pummel each other. But they were too enthusiastic for the play's good. In the process of thrashing and kicking one another, they knocked over one of the oil lamp footlights, setting fire to the flimsy curtains. The flames began to lick the stage's wooden framework. Arthur had to quench them with a chemical fire extinguisher before they could spread.

No one was seriously hurt but the Stanley Jefferson Amateur Dramatic Society was abruptly terminated. Harold demanded that Stan return the white mice. Stan refused but he assured Harold that if the mice had babies he would divide them with him. Whether or not the mice became parents is now lost to history.

Stan lost interest in melodrama, having discovered in boarding school a talent for making people laugh. "I had quite a lisp at the time, my voice was broken, and I wasn't fitting for anything but a comic," Stan later recalled. "So I decided that was my forte."

So he became the class clown at the expense of his studies. But one teacher, a Mr. Bates, appreciated the boy's talent. Stan remembered that "after the kids had gone to bed, Bates would come and take me into his private study where he and a couple of other masters were relaxing….Bates would then have me entertain them with jokes, imitations, what...have you-anything for a laugh...they seemed to get a big kick out of it, and I played many return engagements there."

One night, he impersonated a pompous German master who had the peculiar habit of holding a pencil crosswise in his mouth. According to Stan, "when I couldn't answer his questions in class, he used to go into a frenzy. He'd chew that pencil up into pieces and spit them out of his mouth in disgust." Bates was delighted with his imitation, but the German master wasn't and Stan remembered "he really became my enemy after that."

As he grew older, Stan gradually abandoned his studies to focus on the craft of comedy. When he was fifteen, the Jeffersons moved to Glasgow, Scotland so they'd be near Arthur's mainstay, the Metropole Theatre. Now constantly exposed to the life of the theatre, Stan's desire to perform consumed him. Finally, at sixteen, he left school behind to pursue a career on the stage.

Arthur hoped his son would eventually manage the Metropole Theatre. Stan's older brother Gordon was already pursuing theatre management. At that time, theatre managers didn't need a formal education; just business savvy. Unlike acting, theatre managing provided job security. To groom Stan for this career, Arthur put his son in charge of the gallery box office, counting the money and keeping the records. Through this job, Arthur thought, Stan would learn whether or not the theatre was making a profit, an important skill for a manager.

But Stan was determined to perform. Secretly he spent many hours in front of the bedroom mirror practicing his craft in borrowed make-up and costume. His mother, now retired from the stage because of poor health, knew of Stan's acting aspirations and encouraged them. Madge would regale her son for hours with stories about her stage triumphs and the distinguished actors she worked with.

Stan also told Albert Pickard, a friend of his father's and the proprietor of the Britannia Theatre, of his ambition. Unlike the Metropole Theatre, which specialized in what was known as legitimate theatre, the Britannia showcased music hall entertainment. While legitimate theatre staged complete plays with scenarios, music hall provided a variety of acts- singers, comedians, animals and their trainers, dancers, magicians, etc. Stan pleaded with Mr. Pickard to give him a chance to put on his comedy act, an act he had rehearsed for weeks. To his delight, Mr. Pickard agreed.

Stan needed a costume for his act, so he borrowed his father's new trousers, cut down with patches added, and his father's best frock coat and silk hat. Now the teenager looked like a dignified tramp. But his routine consisted mostly of borrowed gags and quips. Stan later recalled the first joke he presented at his debut at an afternoon matinee:

"Did you hear about the two butterflies? Mmm? The first butterfly was terribly upset. He said to his friend, 'Ohh, I am bothered. I *am* bothered.' 'Why?' asked his chum. The first one said, 'I couldn't go to the dance last week.' 'You couldn't?' said the other butterfly. 'Why ever not?' 'Well,' said the first butterfly, 'I couldn't go because it was a *moth* ball.' "

This joke was not exactly a sterling example of wit. Nevertheless, the audience was delighted with Stan. When he left the stage, he heard shouts of "Encore!" Naturally, he came back on stage, happily basking in the applause. But as Stan bowed, he noticed his father in the audience, panicked, and dropped his hat which rolled toward the footlights. When he tried to catch it, he accidentally kicked the hat into the orchestra pit. One of the musicians, in a rush to retrieve the hat, stepped on it and completely crushed it. Stan fled for the exit but as he ran, he caught Arthur's good frock coat on a steel hook and tore it.

Stan hurriedly took off his make-up and dashed to the Metropole, hoping to avoid his father but Arthur had already gotten there. He called his son to his office and stared silently at him for what seemed like an eternity to Stan. Finally, Arthur said, "Not bad, son, but where on earth did you get those gags?" Stan explained the whole story, expecting his father to chastise him. But Arthur just casually asked him, "Have a whisky and soda?"

Stan was astonished. "But when it dawned on me," Stan later remembered, "I seemed to grow six inches in as many seconds. My boyhood was behind me- Dad was accepting me as a man! Then I did the silliest thing- I burst out crying."

Stan recollected, "...Dad thought I wasn't experienced enough yet to branch out as a single, and suggested I'd be better off with some comedy company...He then secured me an engagement with a very famous company, namely, Levy and Cardwell's Juvenile Pantomimes..." This company specialized in Christmas pantomimes- plays with dialogue based on nursery tales- and toured theatres throughout northern England. At the age of seventeen, Stan debuted in a small role in a production called *Sleeping Beauty- or the Prince with the Golden Key.*

Stan then appeared in another play, *The Gentleman Jockey*. He was also made assistant stage manager. During the day, he would tramp around handing out bills and in the evening, he would help with the baggage as the company arrived to put on shows. In 1908, Stan toured in some comedy sketches with his father's company. One of the sketches was *Home from the Honeymoon* which later inspired two classic Laurel and Hardy films, the silent *Duck Soup* and the talkie *Another Fine Mess*.

Stan then went back to Levy and Cardwell for another Christmas pantomime, *The House That Jack Built*. But on December 1, 1908, just days before this production was about to go on tour, Madge Jefferson passed away. She had never regained her health since she gave birth to her last child when Stan was nine. The exact cause of her death is unknown but it is likely that she died from a respiratory disease that was worsened by Glasgow's industrial smog.

For months, Stan was devastated by his mother's death. According to his second wife Virginia Ruth Rogers, Stan was convinced his father had destroyed her will to live by his infidelities. He had discovered his father was unfaithful years before when he overheard Madge's tearful accusations. Although he admired his father's professional accomplishments, Stan felt personally betrayed. Nevertheless, he had to put aside his grief and bitterness and go on the tour. After all, his boyhood was already behind him.

After *The House That Jack Built* closed in April 1909, Stan decided to create his own solo comedy act. Wearing a battered top hat and brandishing an umbrella, he billed himself as "Young Stanley Jefferson- He of the Funny Ways." But this act bombed with audiences because it blatantly copied the routines of a popular stage comedian named Harry Randall. Stan later said, "I just didn't know what kind of comedian I was. I guess I was at an awkward age. All I know is I enjoyed being in front of the footlights."

To stay in front of the footlights, Stan joined another theatrical company in the summer of 1909. He was assigned a comic role of a policeman in *Alone in the World*, a play that originated in the United States. At least one critic took notice of Stan's performance. Writing for a local paper called *Todmorden Herald*, this reviewer declared, "Mr. Stanley Jefferson...is a first-rate comedian and dancer, and his eccentricities create roars of laughter." Unfortunately, after several months of touring throughout the country, *Alone in the World* was abruptly cancelled before its scheduled gig in Newcastle in October; the manager had skedaddled with the proceeds.

But Stan's luck changed when he met a famous impresario named Fred Karno. This producer was so successful that his comedians performed all over Europe and across the Atlantic in the United States. Karno always had an eye for promising talent. His greatest discovery was a young handsome man named Charlie Chaplin. Chaplin would later become a world renowned film comedian with his persona of a lovable hobo known as the Little Tramp.

In November of 1909, when Karno was staging a pantomime in Glasgow called *Mother Goose*, Stan sneaked backstage during a performance to try to meet him. He looked around furtively as the cast and crew changed costumes and moved props and scenery.

Suddenly, a short, burly man approached him.

"Well Mr. Jefferson Junior," he said to Stan, "What can I do for you?"

Stan said, "I'm looking for Mr. Karno."

The gentleman replied, "You're seeing him now."

Stan was astonished that Karno was so approachable and he found himself telling him of his hopes for a career in comedy.

"Are you funny?" Karno asked. Stan said yes. He may not have known what kind of comedian he was but he knew he could make audiences laugh.

"Very well," Mr. Karno said with a nod, "I'll try you out at 2 pounds [equivalent to around 8 American dollars at the time] a week. Report to Frank O'Neill, who is running my *Mumming Birds* company in Manchester. Push yourself forward, and I'll see you in London in a few weeks' time."

Mumming Birds was a sketch about a play that was constantly disrupted by a drunk in the audience who would loudly insult the amateurish performers. In the sketch's climax, a professional wrestler on stage offered to pay anyone in the theatre who could best him in fifteen seconds. The drunk accepted the offer, tickling the wrestler into submission. The sketch ended with everyone engaged in a battle royal. Stan played most of the roles during its tour but he never got a chance to play the most important part, the drunk. Charlie Chaplin had that role and never missed a performance.

After *Mumming Birds* closed in January 1910, Stan appeared in the supporting cast in another show called *Skating*, starring Chaplin. Then in April of that year, Stan and Chaplin appeared in a new production called *Jimmy the Fearless* about a miner's son who daydreamed he was a dashing hero. Chaplin was supposed to play the title role but during rehearsals he quarreled with Karno and walked off the production. So Stan took Charlie's place. The audience loved him so much that he had to take five curtain calls. Stan was exhilarated to be a "star comedian" in the Karno troupe.

Stan's joy was short-lived. When Chaplin saw the adulation Stan was enjoying, he demanded back the lead. Since Chaplin was Karno's established star, Stan had to give up the title role and return to being Charlie's understudy. It was a terrible blow to Stan but his brief triumph in the lead convinced him that someday he would be famous.

The Fred Karno troupe then staged another show called *The Wow-wows*. After only four performances in England, Fred Karno decided to take the show to North America. On September 22, 1910, the Karno troupe, including Stan and Charlie, sailed from Southampton, England on a converted cattle-boat called *Cairnrona* since commercial air travel was not yet available. After eleven days, the ship docked in Montreal, Quebec, Canada. There, the troupe took a train to New York City to stage the show. Once again, Chaplin was the star while Stan was a supporting player.

Stan later remembered, "We had a lot of fun in those days. Charlie and I roomed together and I can still see him playing the violin or cello to cover the noise of the cooking of bacon I was doing on the gas ring (forbidden of course). Then we'd both take towels and try and blow the smoke out of the window."

One night Stan put his shoes out to be shined, a regular routine in British hotels. The next day, he discovered his shoes were stolen-his only pair! He had to walk to the theater in his bedroom slippers.

The Wow-wows played in New York City until January 1911

but American audiences weren't as enthusiastic as the troupe had hoped. So the group staged a new version of *Mumming Birds* re-titled *A Night in a London Club*, which met with a better reception and went on tour all across the United States and Canada in less than two months.

Stan was unhappy with the tour. Not only was the pace gru-eling, but he had to spend his own money for travel. When the troupe was in Colorado Springs, he demanded a raise from Karno's manager Alf Reeves who flatly turned him down. Stan was learning the hard way that Karno was notoriously stingy with his employ-ees. So he went back to England with another disgruntled member of the Karno troupe, Arthur Dandoe.

There, they developed a sketch with an ancient Roman setting called *The Rum 'Uns from Rome*. This sketch was Stan's first experi-ence in writing comedy; he would become as gifted a writer as he was a performer. But as Stan recalled, "Then, like a couple of silly schoolgirls, Dandoe and I had a slight difference of opinion- and our partnership fizzled out...After that I was out of work for a year." He refused to work for his father because he wanted to strike out on his own.

In 1912, Stan returned to the stage in a show called *The Wax Works* and then revived *The Rum 'Uns* with a new partner, Ted Leo. Then they got together with some other unemployed actors to form an act called "The Eight Comiques." Their tour in the Netherlands and Belgium was a failure so Stan had no choice but to return to England.

Penniless, he had to walk from Waterloo station to his brother

Gordon's flat in High Holoburn. By now, Gordon was thriving as a successful manager of the Princes Theatre in London. Stan had to humble himself and offer his services. Gordon hired him for a small unbilled role in a play there. Now it seemed that Stan's dreams of comedic stardom were doomed. He must have wondered if he would have to take his father's advice and become a theater manager after all.

Then the Fred Karno troupe came to his rescue. When the players returned from North America to England, Alf Reeves ran into Stan and asked him, "What are you doing nowadays? Starring in the West End?" The West End was and still is a prestigious theatre district in London, the British equivalent to New York City's Broadway.

Stan replied, "Starving in the West End, more like it."

Reeves immediately offered to rehire him. To Stan's astonishment, he also offered him the salary raise he had demanded in Colorado Springs. Karno's willingness to give him a raise indicated he knew Stan's worth as an actor. So in the fall of 1912, Stan went on another North American tour with the Karno troupe. Once again, they staged *A Night in a London Club*. And once again, Stan was Charlie Chaplin's understudy.

The troupe was in Philadelphia in May 1913 when Alf Reeves received a telegram from Kessel and Bauman. They had seen Chaplin perform and wanted him to work at Keystone, a comedy film company run by Mack Sennett in California. Charlie thought about this offer for several months. Finally in November, he left the Karno troupe to pursue what would be a remarkable film career.

Suddenly, Stan was the star in the troupe. He could hardly believe his luck. But he didn't remain a star for long. When the company arrived at Philadelphia, they ran into trouble. Karno had signed a twelve-week contract with the city's theatre owners that stipulated Chaplin would be the lead. The troupe's manager tried to assure them that Stan was just as funny as Chaplin. But the owners wouldn't accept Stan in Chaplin's place.

To fulfill the contract, Karno had to bring over a well-known comedian named Dan Raynor from England to star. The troupe waited anxiously for Raynor for three weeks, but when he finally arrived, the show flopped and the troupe broke up. Anybody in the disbanded Karno troupe who wished to return to Britain was given a ticket but Stan decided to stay in the United States.

Once again he had to struggle to find work. In a later interview, he said, "I remember getting a day's work at a vaudeville house doing a shadowgraph act called *Evolution of Fashion*, about a drunk in a cafe. It was almost like a movie- acting in shadow pantomime before a white screen." Vaudeville was the American equivalent to the British music hall, providing a variety of acts like songs, comedy sketches, and physical stunts. The pantomime Stan performed was the standard silent kind, rather than the talking Christmas pantomimes.

Stan then formed a new vaudeville act, *The Nutty Burglars*, with Mr. and Mrs. Edgar Hurley, two other former members of the Karno troupe. For several months, the act played in the Chicago area. When performing in Cleveland, Stan and the Hurleys met two big-time booking agents, Claude and Gordon Bostock.

The Bostocks not only found better bookings for the act but

they revised it, giving it a broader appeal. By now, Charlie Chaplin was a nationally famous film star at Sennett's Keystone studio. Chaplin mania was sweeping the country so Gordon changed the name of the act to the Keystone Trio. Stan imitated Chaplin's Tramp character while the Hurleys imitated Chester Conklin and Mabel Normand, Charlie's co-stars at Keystone. Stan later recalled, "Since Chaplin and I both had the same kind of strong pantomime training, I could do his tramp just as he did it."

But Stan and the Hurleys soon parted. Stan later claimed that Hurley wanted to play the starring Tramp role. He copyrighted the sketch behind Stan's back so only he and his wife could do the sketch and replaced Stan with another actor, Ted Banks. Theatre managers didn't like the new version so the Keystone Trio dissolved.

When Stan was still with the Hurleys, they had shared the bill in St. Thomas, Ontario with a husband-and-wife act, Baldwin and Alice Cooke. Now that Stan was no longer part of the Keystone Trio, he got together with the Cookes to form another act, the Stan Jefferson Trio.

Alice Cooke later recalled, "When Stan first thought of the idea, he said he hadn't had a vacation since he was a little boy and he wanted one. So he had the idea for us to rent a cottage at some beach where we could go swimming and that's where he would write an act for us. We would rehearse every day as well as having a good time, and we'd get that act ready for our fall showing which Claude Bostock...got for us."

After renting a cottage near the Atlantic Highlands in New Jersey, Stan wrote the act and called it *The Crazy Cracksman*. Once again, Stan imitated Chaplin's Little Tramp. For a while, *The Crazy Cracksman* played on the vaudeville circuit. Stan recalled that it was "not the greatest act in the world but it was fun-and anyway, anything for a living!"

It was a happy time for Stan and his partners. Alice Cooke later recalled, "We didn't have ambitions to go on to bigger things. Not us, not Stan either. In those days vaudevillians just lived for fun. That's all we thought of. We lived for fun, food, drinks, and good times...We got $175 a week for our act, which wasn't bad money, and we split it three ways."

They also spent it as soon as they got it. One night when they went out to dinner, they only had enough money for each to have a ham sandwich and two glasses of beer, plus a small tip for the waiter. Just as they finished ordering at a restaurant, Stan spotted a friend and impulsively invited him to join them. Too late he realized he couldn't afford to pay the bill.

Alice then remembered she had a dime bank in her purse. This type of bank needed to hold five dollars before it could open. She knew the bank didn't have five dollars, but it did have *some* money. Baldwin struggled to open it without attracting attention. Using a fork, he picked at the bank under the table. He managed to open it, but he pulled too hard, resulting in four dollars worth of dimes spraying all over the white marble floor and under everyone's table. Baldwin and Stan had to crawl on their hands and knees under all the tables near them to get all the dimes!

Around 1917, the Stan Jefferson Trio played on a bill with a musical act called The Hayden Sisters in a small Pennsylvania town.

The Hayden Sisters weren't actually sisters but were two unrelated women, one of whom was an Australian named Mae Charlotte Dahlberg. Stan became so infatuated with the tall, stately woman that he left *The Crazy Cracksman* to start a new act with her. (He would be reunited with the couple at Hal Roach Studios in the late 1920s and would remain friends with them.) Soon Stan and Mae lived together as common-law husband and wife.

Around this time, he changed his surname to Laurel. "I changed the name on account of billing," he later said. "Jefferson was quite a long name so it always appeared smaller on the billing on that account. So I thought if I had a shorter name, the letters would be bigger..."

Mae later recalled the name change was inspired by an illustration in a history book. In a dressing room during a show, Stan and Mae noticed the book that somebody left behind. In it was a picture of a famous Roman general, Scipio Africanus Major. Around his head he wore a wreath of laurel. Staring at this headpiece, Mae said aloud, "Laurel. Laurel. Stan Laurel."

"What?" Stan asked.

"Laurel, Stan Laurel. How about that for a name?" Mae said.

Stan repeated it aloud. "Stan Laurel. Sounds very good."

So the couple became known on the vaudeville circuit as Stan and Mae Laurel. In the spring of 1917, they performed at the Hippodrome in Los Angeles, California. The theatre's owner, Adolph Ramish, loved Stan's work and felt he had the potential for a great movie career. By now, Hollywood in Los Angeles was quickly replacing New York City as the center of the American movie industry.

Filmmaking was easier in California where the climate was warm and temperate all year round than in New York with its hard winters.

The idea of working in films appealed to Stan and Mae. After all, Charlie Chaplin was already a bigger star in cinema than he ever was on the stage. So Ramish provided the financial backing to make a comedy short subject. Television didn't exist then so short subjects were presented in movie theatres as "added attractions" with the main feature. Shorts were also considered ideal training ground for new film comedians. Charlie Chaplin had started out in movies by appearing in shorts.

Ramish asked Bobby Williamson, an experienced movie co-median and director, to devise a scenario for Stan. The result was a short comedy called *Nuts in May*, in which Stan played a book salesman who thinks he is Napoleon after getting a blow on the head. Mae also appeared in the film but it flopped so the couple went back to vaudeville.

Nevertheless at least one film producer felt Stan would be a hit in movies. Carl Laemmle signed him to a contract with Universal for a series of comedy short subjects but only four were completed. Stan later said that "the films were pretty bad, and were released, so I understand, to all the best comfort stations."

Then in 1918, another producer, Hal Roach, hired Stan to star in a series of comedy shorts. Eventually, Laurel would team up with Oliver Hardy at Roach's studio where they would make their best films. But this was in the future. Stan's first films for Roach were no more successful than the Universal films.

Films were composed of a flammable material called nitrate before 1951. Because of this, many pre-1951 films, including Stan's first film, have disappeared. Of the five films Stan starred in for Roach, only three have survived. But these three movies, *Just Rambling Along*, *Hustling for Health* and *Do You Love Your Wife*, suggest why Stan wasn't going anywhere in films. Charlie Chaplin was a big star because he had an identifiable persona, the endearing Little Tramp. In *Just Rambling Along*, Stan is a thieving scalawag, in *Hustling for Health*, he is a browbeaten yokel, and in *Do You Love Your Wife*, he is a lovesick cretin. If Laurel couldn't maintain a consistent and distinctive characterization, he couldn't make much of an impression on filmgoers and film critics.

Unable to sustain a starring career, Stan signed up at another studio called Vitagraph to support another comedian, Larry Semon. They only worked together on a few films. Stan later claimed that Semon resented him because the film crew found him funnier than the star. For the time being, no more opportunities in Hollywood existed. In the fall of 1918, a great influenza epidemic had resulted in the temporary closing of all the film studios there. Stan had no choice but to return to the stage with Mae.

For a few years, Stan remained in vaudeville. Then in 1921, he tried to re-launch his film career. G.M. "Broncho Billy" Anderson, a cowboy star turned producer, hired Laurel to star in a comedy short for a company called Amalgamated Producing. Entitled *The Lucky Dog*, the short also featured another actor named Oliver Hardy as a villain.

Years later, Stan remembered that on the set of the film he and Hardy were "...friendly, but there was nothing about the picture or our own personal relationship to suggest we might ever become partners. He and I were just two working comics, glad to have a job- any job."

The Lucky Dog made money, so Anderson kept Stan on for a new series of comedy shorts. The first four released films, *The Weak-End Party*, *The Handy Man*, *The Egg*, and *The Pest*, failed to make a big sensation. Laurel still lacked a distinct personality but he didn't need one for the next two films, *Mud and Sand* and *When Knights Were Cold*, which parodied popular features of the day.

Mud and Sand spoofed a bullfighting romance, *Blood and Sand*, starring the dashing and handsome Rudolph Valentino, a matinee idol of the day. Laurel lampooned Valentino's heroics with the jokey name "Rhubarb Vaselino." Critics praised Stan's inspired spoofing. A reviewer in *Motion Picture News* said:

"Every now and then there comes to the screen a young man who 'carries on' idiotically, who appears- casually observed- a mere clowning fool, but who, more thoughtfully considered, shows himself that rarest of artists, a true buffoon, gifted with the power of bringing laughter which is strangely close to tears. Such a man is Charlie Chaplin, and such a man Stan Laurel is by way of becoming fast."

Stan's next film, *When Knights Were Cold*, spoofed *Robin Hood* and *When Knighthood Was in Flower*, contemporary royal costume dramas that captivated moviegoers. The comical character names suggested the film's parodic intent. Stan played Lord Helpus, a Slippery Knight. Other names were Countess Out, a Classy Eve; Earl of Tobasco, a Hot Knight; Duke of Sirloin, a Tough Knight; Rainy Knights, and Foggy Knights.

But by the time this film was released Stan had left Anderson. Despite the critical raves, the movies didn't do as well in return bookings as Laurel and Anderson wished. Once again, Stan returned to vaudeville.

He didn't stay in vaudeville for long. In the spring of 1923, Stan signed up with Hal Roach again. Seven one-reelers (each lasting around ten minutes) were released that year. For the rest of that year, three two-reelers (each lasting around twenty minutes) came out. The following year, Stan starred in eight two-reelers for Roach. He also contributed gags for the shorts.

In these films, Stan generally played a pushy half-wit, a characterization lacking audience appeal. Laughing at his own jokes, he appeared too smug to be funny. But Stan was lucky to have a good foil in these films, a balding saucer-eared Scottish actor named James Finlayson. Although clean-shaven off screen, Finlayson usually sported a bushy mustache in the films. He would comically register incredulity or doubt by performing what he called a "double take and fade away," first slowly expressing surprise and then staring intently with one eye closed.

When Laurel teamed with Hardy, Finlayson would be a valuable nemesis in their films. Indeed, the Scotsman appeared in so many Laurel and Hardy films that he was almost considered a third member of the team. But Finlayson's inspired support in Stan's solo films did not persuade the star to stay with Hal Roach. Laurel left the studio over money disputes in early 1924 and went to work for another producer, Joe Rock.

Rock considered Stan's common-law wife Mae a hindrance. She

insisted on playing Laurel's girlfriend in the films but her severe facial features and imposing stature made her an unsuitable ingenue. Stan threatened to leave if Mae wasn't cast but Rock warned him he could always find another comedian. Finally, Mae agreed to bow out.

Stan's first two films for Rock were financed by the producer's own money. Then Rock obtained a distribution deal with Selznick Distributing Corporation. Laurel devoted all his energies to making these films, showing up early in the morning and remaining on the set until late at night. Not only did Stan act in front of the camera but he also participated in gag sessions. He saw the rushes (movie scenes that had been newly shot) with the rest of the crew and made suggestions afterwards how to improve them. The others on the set respected him for his zeal and talent.

For a while, filmmaking went smoothly. But gradually, Stan's attitude changed. He started showing up late in the morning looking haggard as if he hadn't slept. He also became irritable with the crew and protested having to reshoot scenes. Rock suspected that Mae was the source of Stan's problems. Confronting him, he got Stan to admit that this was the case. Mae was griping that she couldn't work in the films with Stan. She wanted him to quit movies and go back to vaudeville with her. But Stan had no desire to leave Hollywood. He told Rock that Mae was so unhappy in America she would go back to Australia if she could afford it.

Rock had grown fond of Laurel and was anxious to keep him on board, so he arranged to pay for Mae's trip to Australia. Stan became a bachelor again. Now the filmmaking atmosphere was serene and Stan's mood was also serene. Once Mae was gone he felt like a man newly released from jail.

Some of the surviving Joe Rock films remain funny today. In the title role of The *Sleuth*, Stan puts on an amusing series of disguises including one as a mustached gentleman and another as a serving maid. *Dr. Pyckle and Mr. Pryde* risibly spoofs the film version of Robert Louis Stevenson's *Dr. Jekyll and Mr. Hyde* starring John Barrymore. As the fiendish Mr. Pryde, Stan steals an ice-cream from a child and targets passers by with a pea shooter, contorting his face into a hilarious grimace.

Nevertheless, Stan still hadn't found a sturdy characterization at Rock's studio. He also was convinced Rock was underpaying him. Once again Stan became difficult to work with. Finally he decided to leave Rock. To the producer's chagrin, Stan made a deal with Hal Roach. Several films had been completed but were not yet released.

Rock told Stan, "I don't want to stop you from making a living, but if you make anything with Roach, and they're billed as Stan Laurel Comedies, what am I gonna do with my distributors, when *I've* got a deal to deliver Stan Laurel Comedies?"

Laurel said he wanted to go back to the stage. Joe responded, "If you'll put that in writing, it'll be fine." So Stan wrote a letter stating he wouldn't appear in any more films. Rock notified his distributor that no more Laurel comedies would be made.

In May 1925, Laurel began working at Roach as a writer and a director. Though an experienced writer, Stan was a novice at directing. A professional director named F. Richard "Dick" Jones taught him the basics- how to place a camera so the audience could see the action, why a specific shot was most effective in a certain situation.

Soon, Stan had mastered the craft. An Australian comedian, Clyde Cook, remembered being directed by Laurel:

"Stan used to laugh more than anybody else. When he was directing me, he'd say, 'What do you think of this?' and I'd say, 'Well, let's try it.' In one picture, I had to get rid of a body, so I put it on my back and took it out in the country some place. We started to think about what we could do with it. I said, 'What do we do with the body?' And that became a gag with us. When we were stuck for a gag, we asked ourselves, 'What do we do with the body?' "

Another actor that Stan directed was Oliver Hardy. The hefty comedian had arrived at the Roach lot around the same time Laurel had rejoined it as a writer/director. Hardy had been in films longer than Stan had but at this point, he was content to be a supporting player. All that mattered to him was that he was steadily employed. Like Laurel, Hardy had experienced ups and downs in his show business career. But performing was the only job Oliver ever wanted to do. Even when he was a boy named Norvell in Georgia, he would rather entertain people than do anything else. By impressing them with his talent, they wouldn't look down on him as just a fat boy. It was utterly painful for Norvell to be a fat boy.

An Aspiring Actor
From Georgia

Norvell Hardy was born on January 18, 1892 in Harlem, Columbia County, Georgia. His father, Oliver Hardy, was a heavy-set, moon-faced Southern gentleman who had served in the Confederate Army during the Civil War. Georgia was one of eleven Southern states that seceded from the United States in 1861 after Abraham Lincoln won the U.S. Presidential election of 1860. Lincoln led the Republican Party, which opposed slavery. The Republican Party's main support came from Northern industrial states where slavery was outlawed.

Georgia, like other Southern states, depended on black slave labor for its plantation-based economies. Mr. Hardy himself owned slaves. The white Georgians feared that Lincoln would force them to free their slaves so Georgia declared itself part of a new nation called the Confederate States of America.

The Southern states' secession from the Union resulted in the Civil War. As a sergeant in the Confederate Army, Oliver Hardy fought bravely and was wounded at the Battle of Antietam. The Southern states lost the war in 1865 and slavery was abolished all over the country.

It took years for Georgia to recover from this defeat. From 1865 to 1870, federal troops occupied the state to reconstruct its economy and society. The Georgians gradually adjusted to life without slavery, although the freed blacks would not enjoy the same civil rights as the whites until the 1960s.

Oliver Hardy also adjusted to this new life, rising to become a local politician and Tax Collector in Columbia County. He developed a reputation as a warm, jovial fellow who charmed ladies and babies. Despite his girth, Hardy had the refinement, charm, and agility of a dancing instructor.

Oliver was married and widowed twice and fathered three children before he wed Norvell's mother, Emily Norvell. A native Georgian with a hefty build like her husband, Emily was a widow with four children. By the time Norvell was born, Oliver had long ago departed his Tax Collector's office and was now running a hotel in Madison, Morgan County, Georgia.

Although Norvell was born in Harlem he spent his infancy and early childhood in Madison. On November 22, 1892, when he was only ten months old, his father died at forty-seven. Norvell cherished his mother's stories about him and when he was a teenager, he added "Oliver" to his name.

Because her husband did not leave a valid will, Emily had to apply to the court for guardianship of Norvell; in those days, women had few rights. The court gave her custody of the baby as well as $628 out of the deceased's property for one year's support but the hotel owners wouldn't let Emily take over her husband's job. Undaunted, she established a new hotel called the Hardy House, gaining a reputation as a genial landlady.

But it wasn't easy for Emily to maintain her business and eventually she had to give up the Hardy House to the owners of Turnell-Butlier. She found work in a boarding house in Madison and then at a hotel in Athens. When Norvell was about eight, the family moved to the state capital of Atlanta, but life was still difficult there. One Christmas, Emily could not buy her children a single present. Trying to start again, she moved the family to Milledgeville and began operating another hotel called the Baldwin.

Because Emily was occupied with her work, Norvell rarely saw his mother in his early years. Like many white children in the South, he was cared for by a black female servant called a "mammy." When Novell did see his mother, he addressed her as "Miss Emmie," another Southern tradition.

Norvell was fat from infancy, weighing fourteen pounds at birth. He probably inherited his corpulence from his father and must have appeared almost grotesque to people. Still he could charm them with a beautiful soprano voice. Norvell would sit at the piano in the Baldwin and sing for relatives and visitors, particularly two popular songs of the day, "Silver Threads Among the Gold" and "When You and I Were Young, Maggie."

When he wasn't singing or going to school, Norvell was given tasks at the hotel. One arduous assignment embarrassed the boy. He would be sent out into the streets of Milledgeville carrying a sandwich board that advertised the Baldwin Hotel's menu. For an obese child already self-conscious about his appearance, this was humiliating.

Norvell enjoyed people watching in the hotel lobby. Years later when he became a successful comedian, he said, "Whenever

I travel, I still am in the habit of sitting in the lobby and watching the people walk by- and I tell you I see many Laurels and Hardys. I used to see them in my mother's hotel when I was a kid: the dumb, dumb guy...and the smart, smart guy who's dumber than the dumb guy only he doesn't know it."

Occasionally, the boy would travel over seventy-five miles to Atlanta to see a stage show. To help pay for these trips, Norvell used the tips he earned as a porter in the Baldwin Hotel. Once he saved enough money to buy a cheap ticket for an Atlanta production of the popular operetta *The Bohemian Girl*. Norvell didn't have enough money for the fare home so he walked most of the way back, riding the last six miles on a friendly farmer's wagon.

On another trip to Atlanta, he saw the famous opera tenor Enrico Caruso. Norvell had heard the tenor's voice on phonograph records. Unlike today's compact discs, phonograph records in the early twentieth century sounded hollow and scratchy so Caruso's recordings didn't impress the boy. He was astounded to hear the tenor in person. Hardy later recalled this experience as the single greatest musical event in his entire life and it convinced him that singing was his destiny.

The youth became so obsessed with music that he began neglecting his studies. A concerned Miss Emmie sent her son to a boarding school north of Atlanta. But Norvell soon became unhappy there and at the age of fourteen, he ran away to Atlanta.

On the same day Norvell arrived in Atlanta, an ugly race riot erupted. Often whites in Georgia and other southern states would accuse blacks of not knowing their place and physically attack them and destroy their property. It must have been frightening for

Norvell to come upon a scene of such violence and hatred.

Then it started to rain heavily and he was caught in a downpour. Norvell found himself plodding along a deserted road, a foot deep in red mud but managed to follow a railroad track to the Atlanta depot. There, a friendly stationmaster helped him to get cleaned up and then alerted his mother. Although it was still raining, Norvell walked all the way back to Milledgeville. "I was," he later recalled, "quite a remarkable sight."

Realizing that her son's true love was singing, Miss Emmie sent him to the Atlanta Conservatory of Music but Norvell found the vocal training there to be grueling. A job offer at a movie house near the Conservatory was more appealing. At this time, movie houses showed illustrated slides which displayed the lyrics of popular songs. Someone would sing the lyrics while the slides were displayed. Because of his magnificent singing voice, Norvell was hired at $3.50 a week.

In the early twentieth century, $3.50 a week was a significant amount of money but to earn it Norvell had to cut classes at the Conservatory. When Miss Emmie went to Atlanta to check her son's academic progress, she learned that he hadn't attended the school for weeks. She made Norvell go back to the Conservatory, although she allowed him to sing at the movie house on weekends.

Soon Norvell neglected his studies again. This time, Miss Emmie took him out of the Conservatory and sent him to a military school, Georgia Military College, in Milledgeville. It was across the street from the Baldwin Hotel so she could keep an eye on him. Military school was an agonizing experience for Norvell. He had always been conscious of being overweight, but to be fat in a military school, where physical trimness was essential, was especially humiliating. He also hated the school's rigid discipline, particularly the drills. Once during an exercise, he became so tired, he collapsed to the ground and refused to move when he was ordered to stand up. Nobody could carry the obese Norvell off the parade ground. He lay there until he felt he was finally able to get himself up!

A voracious eater, Norvell felt there was never enough food at the school and he was always hungry. One day, feeling famished, he ran across the street to his mother's hotel. Norvell told Miss Emmie he would only go back if she prepared some of his favorite baking powder biscuits. It took twenty big biscuits to satisfy him.

Norvell tried to deal with the military school's rigors by becoming a class clown. The headmaster encouraged the youth's comical antics, realizing that clowning was therapeutic for Norvell. At a commencement exercise, the youth participated in a staged skit based on an old folk song, "Who Killed Cock Robin?" The skit's climax was the singing of the title song by most of the cast in chorus. Norvell admitted his guilt in a hefty bull's costume. He sang out in a melodious voice that contradicted his brutish appearance:

I killed Cock Robin!
I tolled the bell because
I could pull the rope.
I am the bull!

Hitting a high C on the final word, Norvell convulsed the audience. The headmaster later told him that he was "the funniest boy in the world."

Despite this triumph, Norvell still detested Georgia Military

College. He begged Miss Emmie to send him away to "any other place." She relented and sent him to Young Harris College, a high school and college in the high hills of northern Georgia, which provided outdoor activities as well as academic work.

At Young Harris, Norvell was popular with both the students and the faculty. When going on an assigned camping expedition through the Georgian hills, he amused his peers with a comical impersonation. Pretending to be a rural mountaineer, Norvell pantomimed a rustic walk. Approaching a tree, he feigned terror at witnessing a bear. Norvell quickly climbed the tree and at the top looked down at the imaginary creature. In a faultless Georgia mountain-man accent, he yelled, "Lawd, if you don't help me, don't help that bear!"

Norvell soon lost interest in his studies at Young Harris. He briefly thought about law school and mentioned it to his family. But his older half sister Elizabeth convinced him that the law was not for him. "Norvell honey," she said, "you're just a big, fat baby. How'd you ever win a lawsuit?"

Norvell decided to quit school in order to pursue a show business career and got a job at a theatre called the Milledgeville Opera House. Despite its grand name, this theatre didn't show operas but vaudeville. Norville became a stand-in, singing whenever a scheduled act was unavailable. The Milledgeville townspeople enjoyed watching one of their fellow residents performing, and so well at that.

Vaudeville was a great diversion for the Milledgeville community. But when Norvell was around eighteen, a new source of entertainment showed up in the town- motion pictures. Although they were primitively crafted, they were becoming very popular all over the United States. A local businessman opened the first movie theatre across the street from the Opera House, called the Electric Theatre.

The Electric Theatre fascinated Norvell so he got a job there operating the projector that screened the films. He also had other duties- taking tickets, sweeping out the theatre, singing to illustrated slides as he did in Atlanta, and acting as manager when his boss was gone. The moviegoers found him a buoyant presence, joking and bantering with them as he took the tickets. As the people left, Norvell would always say to them, "Come back now, hear?"

The usual program at a movie theatre in the early 1910s included a two-reel (around twenty minutes) drama or adventure, a one-reel (around ten minutes) western, a one-reel comedy, and an educational reel. Norvell found himself emotionally involved with the dramas, cheering the heroes, hissing the villains, despairing over the plot crises and rejoicing at the happy endings. He found the comedians to be a mixed bag. Some he thought were outstanding, particularly a French comedian named Max Linder who played the part of a sophisticated gentleman with a top hat, thin mustache, and cane in his films. Max would endure comic indignities but he was always confident he would triumph in the end. Charlie Chaplin's Little Tramp, who was also blessed with self-assurance despite his own problems, was influenced by Linder's screen character.

He found other comedies unremarkable. The gags weren't funny and the performers weren't appealing. Norvell became interested in doing comedy himself. He later recalled, "...I thought to myself that

I could be as good- or maybe as *bad*- as some of those boys."

For about two years, he worked at the Electric Theatre. By now, he had added "Oliver" to his name. Then he learned about a flourishing filmmaking colony in Jacksonville, Florida from a friend who had vacationed there. At that time, Florida was considered an ideal filmmaking environment because the weather was warm and sunny all year round. Eager to join this filmmaking colony, Oliver quit his job when he was twenty-one and traveled to Jacksonville.

At first he had to support himself in Jacksonville by singing in vaudeville and nightclubs at night. Oliver decided to exploit his girth by billing himself as "The Ton of Jollity." He then returned to his home state, bringing his singing act to the Montgomery Theatre in Atlanta. At the same theatre was a pianist named Madelyn Saloshin. Although plain in appearance, she had a lively personality that captivated Oliver. The attraction was mutual and on November 17, 1913, they got married. Soon they moved back to Jacksonville.

There, Oliver performed on stage almost exclusively at night. In the daytime, he usually visited the film studios, studying how they operated. One particular studio he would frequent was the Lubin Film Company. Since tourists could wander on the studio's exterior stage, Oliver watched the activities of the comedy players. He was eager to be near them because they seemed to be having so much fun so he volunteered to be the company water boy.

One day, a Lubin director asked him if he was available for the studio's next comedy because a fat man was needed. Heavy people were already considered assets in film comedies. Their enormous bulk guaranteed that they would be effective as villains or buffoons.

Indeed, two hefty performers, John Bunny and Roscoe "Fatty" Arbuckle, were popular comedy stars.

Oliver gladly accepted the offer. On April 21, 1914, Hardy's first film, *Outwitting Dad*, was released. Lubin was impressed with him so the studio hired him at five dollars a day with a contract for three days' work each week. Soon after Hardy began working in films, he acquired a new nickname. Near the Lubin studio was a barbershop run by a friendly Italian named Enzo. When he would rub talc into Hardy's plump, newly shaven cheeks, he would say in a thick accent, "Nice-a babe-e-e. Nice-a babe-e-e!" The other Lubin actors started calling Oliver "Baby" and then shortened it to "Babe." Friends would refer to Hardy by that nickname for the rest of his life.

The Lubin comedies that Oliver appeared in were generally issued in "split-reels"- two comedies of varying length on the same reel. Occasionally, Hardy acted in a complete reel devoted to one comedy. He played all kinds of roles in these films- a policeman, a cowboy, a sailor, a convict, a bartender, a cook, even a female role in drag. In whatever part he played, Hardy distinguished himself. Despite his weight, Oliver was physically agile and graceful. A fellow Lubin actor and friend, Bert Tracey, later said to Hardy's biographer John McCabe:

"Now mind you, any fairly good actor or comic can do a take well enough. A take is just a very big reaction to something. It is an over-reaction, really...The average comic does the take mostly with his face, and it can be quite funny, serving its purpose of helping build up the laugh. But Babe did takes with his whole body, not just his face or shoulders the way most comics do it."

The Lubin studio appreciated Oliver's talent. Soon it advertised him: "Babe Hardy, the funniest fat comedian in the world, is in all these subjects.- He's a fair knockout." But Babe wouldn't stay at Lubin much longer.

In February 1915, the studio in Jacksonville closed. Looking for work elsewhere, Hardy took a steamer to New York City. The trip was a nightmare for him because he was horribly seasick and became severely sunburned from spending a lot of time on deck. His lips in particular were affected, terribly puffed up and swollen. To his torment, Babe couldn't eat.

When he arrived in New York City, Babe, not sure how long he would be out of work, chose an inexpensive hotel called the Mills. By the time he got there after midnight, he discovered that the elevator had stopped running. He had to walk twenty stories to a very shabby room. Babe only spent three days in the city, finding New York unsettling and chaotic, particularly its clamorous traffic. He returned to Jacksonville, this time taking the train.

For a while he remained in Florida. But following Bert Tracey's advice, he went back to New York City where film jobs were more plentiful. He found work in several film studios- Edison, Wharton, Pathe, Gaumont, Mittenthal, Novelty, and Wizard. Even though he didn't care for New York City, he must have relished the food there because in a surviving film *Something in Her Eye*, he looks heavier than he did in the extant Lubin pictures.

Although Babe enjoyed working in films, his greatest desire at this point was to be a singer on the vaudeville circuit. But booking agents considered him to be an anomaly, an enormous man with a heavenly voice. To them, these two characteristics did not seem to blend. Babe realized this didn't matter in Florida where there was less competition. Besides, the weather was much more pleasant there than in New York City so Babe returned to Jacksonville.

There Babe not only resumed his singing career in cabaret, but he also found work at a new film studio. The Vim Comedy Company, whose headquarters were in New York City, had established a studio in Jacksonville. To Babe's delight, the studio operated only in the daytime. Thus, he could perform in the cabaret at night and earn extra money. His wife Madelyn became director of an orchestra at the Burbidge Hotel Cabaret. This orchestra specialized in a musical forerunner to jazz called ragtime. There, Babe became part of a singing quartet, variously named "The Twentieth Century Four," "The Half Ton of Harmony," and the old billing "The Ton of Jollity." He was so popular at the hotel that he was soon placed in charge of all entertainment.

With his new success, Babe felt that now he could afford to help people out. He would oblige anyone who asked him for money. Often they didn't repay him but Babe was too tenderhearted to press the issue. He soon acquired a reputation as "the original Mr. Soft Touch."

At Vim, Babe was teamed with another performer, Billy Ruge, to star in a series of comedy shorts called "Plump and Runt." Unsurprisingly, Hardy played Plump. These were frenetic slapstick films that called for a lot of physical action. As at Lubin, Babe was more than up to the task, particularly evident in a scene from an extant film, *One Too Many*. As his biographer John McCabe describes the moment: "Trying to quiet his nerves, he prepares to drink off a quick shot of liquor. Holding the glass a foot and a half in front of him, he jerks it up slightly, forcing the liquor to leave the glass in an extended high-arc parabola into his mouth. The liquor does no such thing, of course- there is none there- but the dexterity of his motion tells us it does, his pantomime convincing us we see what we do not."

The atmosphere at Vim was friendly and easygoing. There was no hierarchy among those involved in the filmmaking, so Babe directed some films for the studio. But he soon learned something troubling about the company. Vim's actors were paid in cash in envelopes every Saturday. The salaries were confidential so nobody asked each other what they received. Babe discovered the salary list and realized the Florida office wasn't paying the actors the full amount it received from the New York office. Enraged, Hardy confronted the head and demanded, "Hey...you're only paying me so much, but you're charging the guy in New York to pay a lot more."

When the news became public, it spelled the end for Vim. The studio's co-founders, executive Mark Dintenfass and lawyer Louis Burstein, sued each other. Then at the end of 1916, Vim ceased operations on the orders of its parent company, Amber Star. A new film company, the King Bee Film Corporation, took over Vim's studios. Along with other former Vim players, Babe joined King Bee.

The star of King Bee's comedies was a Russian-born comedian named Billy West. Just as Stan Laurel had done in vaudeville, West impersonated Charlie Chaplin's Little Tramp. At this time, the real

Chaplin only made four shorts a year, because he spent a great deal of money and time to make them perfect. The moviegoing public eagerly accepted Billy West's imitations while waiting for the next Chaplin short. Charlie Chaplin had a heavy-set nemesis with bushy eyebrows played by Eric Campbell. So in Billy West's comedies, the heavy-set Babe was fitted with similar looking eyebrows to resemble Campbell.

After producing some Billy West comedies in Jacksonville, the King Bee Company moved to Bayonne, New Jersey in 1917. Around this time, the United States entered World War I, then known as the Great War. A patriotic Babe rushed to the nearest recruiting office. But when he told the officer in charge he wished to enlist, he received no answer.

Instead, the officer stared at Babe's obese frame. He yelled into another office, "Hey, Sarge, come and look at what wants to enlist."

The two officers looked at Babe and started laughing and wise-cracking. The actor felt pained and humiliated. All his dreams of wartime heroism were shattered.

Fortunately, Babe's movie career nursed his bruised ego. In the fall of 1917, the King Bee Company relocated to Hollywood, California. Babe took a special Pullman carriage on the Santa Fe Sunset Flyer and arrived there on October 24.

Babe enjoyed the California climate because it was warm and temperate like in the South. He would live there for the rest of his life. For a while he continued to support Billy West in King Bee comedies until the company, having over-extended itself, went out of business. So in the summer of 1918, Babe worked at another film studio Lehrman-Knock Out, or L-KO for short. It wasn't long before L-KO also went out of business.

L-KO had released the films through another studio called Vitagraph. Babe found a job at that studio supporting a comedy star named Jimmy Aubrey. Like Laurel, Aubrey was a veteran of the Fred Karno troupe. An egomaniac, he envied and resented Babe's talent. Aubrey wanted him out, but the star's director, Jess Robbins, defended Hardy. The star, anxious to remain in Robbins' good graces, excessively fawned at Babe's feet. Hardy wasn't fooled but he was too much of a gentleman to get angry.

For a few years, Hardy worked in Aubrey's films. He was gaining a reputation in Hollywood as a reliable performer who always enriched his assigned role and showed boundless energy in slapstick capers.

"Some of those guys I worked with," he later recalled, "would get pretty winded. But I took it all in stride because I looked on it as a kind of game, just as if I were out on the football field. I loved my work and I like to think that showed up on the screen."

In 1921, Hardy's stint in Aubrey comedies ended. He began supporting Larry Semon, a more prestigious comedy star at Vitagraph. Laurel may have felt that Semon was jealous of him, but Hardy never had the same problem. The surviving Semon films reveal that Babe could showcase his comedic gifts. Semon also valued Babe as a production assistant. He would occasionally ask for Hardy's views on gag construction and to work behind the camera. In a few films, Babe was credited as assistant director.

Hardy and Semon became personal friends as well. Semon introduced him to golf which became his lifelong passion. Babe once explained in an interview, "I love it because it's social...-nothing is quite like a good foursome of nice guys enjoying each other's company. And it's challenging...without a whole lot of fuss." Eventually, he became known as one of the best golfers in the Hollywood industry.

The same year that Babe began working with Semon, he divorced Madelyn after being estranged for some time. It is lost to history why Oliver fell out of love with Madelyn. But judging by the existing legal records, their divorce wasn't friendly. In later years Oliver preferred to forget this unpleasant episode and never spoke of it.

A week after the divorce he remarried on Thanksgiving Day. His new bride, Myrtle Reeves, was an actress from his home state of Georgia. Oliver had courted her for several years. After the wedding, the couple went on an extended honeymoon. For a while, Babe was able to support his wife by appearing in Larry Semon comedies.

Semon lavishly spent both time and money on the films. He worked on one comedy, *The Sawmill*, for three months. Filming it on location in the mountains, he had log cabins built for the crew and cast. Because of the high costs, the films didn't make a profit. Soon Vitagraph informed Semon the studio would no longer finance his comedies and he would have to raise his own funds.

After producing a few more films with the usual excessive budgets, Semon learned in early 1923 that Vitagraph refused to release any more of them. This decision temporarily put Semon and Babe out of work and for a while, Hardy disappeared from movies. He was hired as an assistant director and gag man on a feature called *Quicksand*, but otherwise he was unemployed.

By mid 1924, Babe was working in front of the cameras again. Larry Semon had established his own company, Chadwick Pictures Corporation, and hired Hardy to appear in his new films. Now Semon was producing and starring in features. His most ambitious project was an adaptation of L. Frank Baum's *The Wonderful Wizard of Oz*. Semon played the Scarecrow while Hardy was the Tin Woodsman. But *The Wizard of Oz*, released in 1925, hardly resembled the classic story and flopped at the box office. Soon Semon's company collapsed, he filed for bankruptcy, and he died in 1928 at only thirty-nine.

Babe no longer had to depend on Semon for work. He appeared in some comedy shorts for a studio called Arrow Pictures. In one film, *Stick Around*, he played an early version of the pompous fool who would enchant audiences as part of the team of Laurel and Hardy. Like his later, more famous character, Babe sported a derby and a little mustache. He bossed around another performer, Bobby Ray, as he would boss around Laurel in the future.

Then in 1925, Hardy started working on a free-lance basis at Hal Roach Studios. When he wasn't at Roach, Hardy appeared in Larry Semon films and in films produced by the Fox Studio. He even acted in a film produced by Mack Sennett, *Crazy to Act*. Sennett had been a pioneering comedy producer whose studio Keystone had starred Charlie Chaplin in films a decade earlier.

But by the mid 1920s, Hal Roach was a serious rival to Sennett. Roach's comedies were more sophisticated than Sennett's, with stronger plots and sturdier characterizations. On February 6, 1926, Hardy signed a long-term contract with Roach. In reporting this, the Los Angeles *Times* noted that he would "play various types of supporting roles...with the prospect eventually of being featured in his own right." What nobody knew at the time was that Babe would soon become one of Roach's greatest stars, as a member of an amazing duo.

The Birth of a
Beautiful Partnership

Hal Roach Studios was an ideal environment to make film comedies. Unlike other studio moguls, Roach allowed his filmmakers creative freedom and leisurely schedules to make their comedies as good as possible. As was the case at Vim, there was no hierarchy among the cast and crew. Whether one was a star or a script clerk, he or she was treated as an equal. Anyone with any good ideas for a film could contribute. Anyone could also speak his or her mind without fear of getting into trouble.

Because of the lack of caste and regimentation, the atmosphere on the lot was convivial. Everyone greeted each other and addressed each other by name. On a set, other actors would drop by. Production halted for fun and games and casually resumed after a half an hour. With everyone in good spirits, it was easy to make humorous pictures. The studio became known as the Lot of Fun.

Hal Roach himself was quite genial for a studio mogul. Richard Currier, who was head of the studio's film editing department from 1920 to 1932, said, "I've never heard of anybody that didn't like Hal Roach...He was friendlier than other bosses at the studios. He was the big boss, but he didn't show it."

Stan Laurel certainly enjoyed writing and directing for Hal Roach. He would have probably remained behind the camera at the studio if an accident hadn't forced him in front of it again. Ironically, the actor Stan had to replace was Oliver Hardy.

In the summer of 1926, Stan planned to direct a comedy called *Get 'Em Young*. Babe was supposed to play a timid butler in that film. One night, Hardy tried to cook a leg of lamb because his wife Myrtle was in bed with an injured leg. He spilled scalding grease from a frying pan over his right hand and wrist. Then he slipped and fell, twisting his leg and bruising himself.

There was little time to find a replacement for Hardy. Dick Jones, who supervised production of the Roach films, begged Stan to take over Babe's role but he refused. At this point, Stan found writing and directing more satisfactory than acting. And if he did appear in front of the screen, he'd violate his promise to Joe Rock that after leaving his studio, he wouldn't perform anymore.

Finally, Roach himself convinced Stan to play the butler when he offered him a $100 raise. Fred Guiol took over directing duties. Although Laurel continued to write and direct, his appearance in *Get 'Em Young* reinvigorated his acting career. (Roach and Rock sued each other over the issue of Laurel performing in front of the camera. By the end of 1926, the dispute was resolved and Rock permitted Stan, in writing, to act in Roach's films.)

Meanwhile, Stan appeared with Babe for the first time in a Roach picture, *45 Minutes from Hollywood*. But no one could decide if they had any chemistry because they didn't share any scenes.

Then Laurel and Hardy acted as a team in their next film together, *Duck Soup*. Watching the film, Richard Currier and Dick Jones observed how well Stan and Babe worked with each other.

Currier asked Jones, "How about taking this guy, Hardy, and letting him be the foil for Laurel?'"

Jones replied, "You know something, I was thinking the same thing."

Laurel and Hardy work fabulously together in *Duck Soup*, performing as if they've been partners for years. For a start, they *look* funny. Hardy's pudgy frame humorously contrasts with Laurel's comparatively angular build. They also have vivid personalities; Stan's vapidity and Oliver's pomposity complement each other. Laurel and Hardy don't have to strictly rely on gags for laughs. Their characterizations provide much of *Duck Soup*'s comedy.

Despite Currier and Jones' opinions, most of the people on the Roach lot, including the comedians themselves, saw the partnership in *Duck Soup* as a one-shot project. In the following films Laurel and Hardy worked on- *Slipping Wives, Love 'Em and Weep, Why Girls Love Sailors, With Love and Hisses,* and *Sailors, Beware!*- they were not a team. In some of these films, Stan and Ollie played enemies. In *Slipping Wives*, Hardy's character hates Laurel's character so much, he tries to kill him!

Nevertheless Stan and Ollie's continued appearances together in films showed that the Roach crew saw the rapport between them and no one had forgotten what a fine duo they had been in *Duck Soup*. In the spring of 1927, Laurel and Hardy were partners again when they played the title roles in *Do Detectives Think?* In this film, they wore black derby hats like movie and real-life detectives at the time. The derbies would become a familiar trademark, as would the rumpled suits and ties they wore in the short. All these articles of clothing gave them an air of battered dignity.

Laurel and Hardy's characterizations are further developed in *Do Detectives Think?* Stan's character is less aggressive than in *Duck Soup*, conveying a more tranquil- and charming- dumbness than in his solo films. Babe's character is more refined in his behavior than he was in *Duck Soup* as he infuses his self-importance with elegance and charm. Both performers project warmth, making them endearing as well as funny. The partnership itself is captivating, two innocents who only have each other in a hostile world.

The partnership was not yet official. In the following two films, *Flying Elephants* and *Sugar Daddies*, Laurel and Hardy were merely two actors who happened to be in the same film. It took the initiative of a gregarious director named Leo McCarey to make Stan and Babe a permanent team.

Leo McCarey had a reputation as a comedic genius on the Roach lot. He greatly influenced the studio's sophisticated humor; particularly evident when he directed a series of comedies starring a tall, handsome, mustached actor, Charley Chase, from 1924 to 1926. The focus in these films was on Chase's persona as a lovable Everyman who got into farcical yet reasonably credible situations. Unlike comedies at other studios, the humor arose from the character and the situations rather than from isolated gags. In 1926, McCarey was promoted to production supervisor. Impressed with Laurel and Hardy's chemistry, he decided to develop the comedians' partnership.

Stan Laurel initially opposed the idea. He didn't dislike Babe but to team with him meant a long-term commitment as an actor. Stan wanted to return to full-time directing and writing as soon as possible. On the other hand, Babe was eager to be part of a team because it would make him a star. Hal Roach agreed with Babe and McCarey about permanently teaming the two comedians. Stan resigned himself to this situation.

And so a glorious era in film history began when the first official Laurel and Hardy film, *The Second Hundred Years*, was released in October 1927. The studio's publicity department announced this new team's birth: "New starring team uncorks riotous performance in first picture as comedy duo. The super comedy arrives!" Press releases, then and now, have been notorious for stretching the truth, but this one was one hundred percent accurate. In this short, Laurel and Hardy play escaped convicts who masquerade as street painters and then as prison officials visiting the same jail they broke out of- with hilarious results. The comedians perform in a slower pace than they did in their previous team efforts, ideally suiting their characters- Stan's serene simpleton and Ollie's pompous yet refined buffoon. This film also spotlights their naivete. In his review of *Second Hundred Years* on his website, Leave 'em Laughing, Steven Bailey cites the scene where they try to pass off as painters: "they act like little kids who announce 'I'm a painter' and demonstrate their expertise by acting like Picassos [Pablo Picasso was a famous artist] wherever they go--a perfect demonstration of their child-like qualities."

Justifiably proud of this new team, Hal Roach employed Stan

and Ollie in cameo roles in *Call of the Cuckoos*, starring another comedian, Max Davidson. In their next starring film, *Hats Off*, Stan sported his trademark upraised haircut for the first time. This hairstyle emerged by accident. For *Second Hundred Years*, both Stan and Babe's heads were shaved so they'd resemble convicts. By the time filming began for *Hats Off*, their hair began to grow in. One day, Stan tried to brush his hair back but he couldn't prevent it from sticking up. Everyone on the lot laughed at his appearance. Stan decided this wacky hairstyle was appropriate for his character, so he flaunted it in most of the subsequent Laurel and Hardy films.

Unfortunately, no copies of *Hats Off* are known to exist. But judging from contemporary reviews, both audiences and critics loved the team. Harrison Carroll of the *Los Angeles Evening Herald* wrote: "I laughed so hard I cried...It is no exaggeration to say that the entire audience bordered on hysteria at the climax of this two-reeler...In my opinion, Hal Roach has the most promising comedy team on the screen today in Laurel and Hardy."

In still photographs from *Hats Off*, Laurel and Hardy are wearing their trademark derbies and suits. But in their next film, the comedians looked and acted differently. In *Putting Pants on Philip*, Babe played a haughty straw-hatted gentleman named Piedmont Mumblethunder and Stan played Mumbelthunder's Scottish kilt-wearing, girl-chasing nephew Philip. As their roles suggested, their relationship was like that between a superior and a subordinate rather than two peers. But elements of these roles- for example, Laurel's humorous crying and Hardy's attempts to preserve his authority and dignity despite comedic chaos- would be used to enrich their characterizations in subsequent pictures.

The following film, *The Battle of the Century*, found Stan and Ollie once again in derbies and suits and behaving like partners. The elaborate pie-throwing melee in the climax distinguishes this film. Pie throwing had been a staple of film comedies ever since the previous decade when it originated in Mack Sennett's Keystone comedies. By 1927, it had become a cliche. Still devising gags behind the scenes despite his new star status, Stan suggested this film should *parody* the concept of pie throwing. Up to this time, a pie was only hurled once at a single individual in film comedies. Stan proposed that a countless number of pies should be hurled at countless individuals. He later explained how the Roach crew executed this concept: "It wasn't just that we threw hundreds of pies. That wouldn't have been very funny; it really *had* passed out with Keystone. We went at it, strange as it may sound, psychologically. We made every one of the pies count.

"A well-dressed man strolling casually down the avenue, struck squarely in the face by a large pastry, would not proceed at once to gnash his teeth, wave his arms in the air and leap up and down. His first reaction, it is reasonable to suppose, would be one of numb disbelief," he went on. "Then embarrassment, and a quick survey of the damage done to his person. Then indignation and a desire for revenge would possess him; if he saw another pie close at hand, still unspoiled, he would grab it up and let fly."

The pie fight exemplified what would be a staple in subsequent Laurel and Hardy films- reciprocal destruction or "tit-for-tat." This battle would modestly begin with a skirmish. As tempers heated up, Stan, Ollie, and their antagonist would devise more extreme methods to humiliate each other, or else more people would get involved in the conflict. The humor derived not only from the comical destruction but the combatants' reactions. Tit-for-tat could be employed in any situation. For instance, in the climax of a later Laurel and Hardy film, *You're Darn Tootin'*, people kicked each other's shins and tore each other's pants off. In another Laurel and Hardy film, *Two Tars*, cars were demolished.

By the time *Battle of the Century* was released, Laurel and Hardy were established stars at Hal Roach's studio. In the following year, they maintained their popularity without sacrificing their artistic integrity. Because Roach provided the crew and cast with enough time and money to meticulously craft the films, the quality was remarkably high. Leo McCarey continued to supervise the films until December 1928 when he left the Roach lot. As for Stan, he continued to work behind the scenes to ensure the films' funniness.

Although Stan wasn't credited as such, he was actually the head writer. After listening to gag men's suggestions, he would add his own ideas and would distill them in the final script. Being a modest man, he never was listed as director in the films but he always collaborated with the official director. The director always treated Stan as an equal and never overruled his objections.

"A lot of directors thought they were directing Stan," Anita Garvin, an actress in Roach films, said, "but believe me, Stan was the one who was directing. And the director was never cognizant of the fact. Stan was clever; he had a brain, in spite of that [vapid onscreen] look. He would make suggestions in such a clever way. He'd say, 'You started to say...' And the director thought it was his own idea.

"He'd suggest different things to the actors, too. He'd say, 'How do you think this would work?' He wouldn't tell you what to do, but he'd ask your opinion. And 99% of the time, you'd say 'Great!'- because he had a comedy mind like no one I have ever known, before or since."

Even Leo McCarey, who later enhanced his reputation as a comedic wizard with such renowned films like *Duck Soup* (an entirely different film, starring the Marx Brothers) and *The Awful Truth*, treated Stan as a partner, rather than as a subordinate. He later recalled that after shooting was finished, Laurel would work on gags and story or help him cut the picture. Such was Stan's talent and drive that when McCarey left Roach, Laurel took over supervising the Laurel and Hardy films.

Babe was not as involved with production behind the camera as Stan. Despite his directing experience, he didn't believe he had the necessary talent. Babe would examine the scripts and if he found any lines that he felt were out of character, he would comment. But when shooting was finished, he would leave the lot to play golf or bet on horses at the racetrack. Babe respected Laurel's artistic judgement. Whenever anyone asked him about the team's plans for an upcoming picture, he would often reply, "Ask Stan."

Under Stan's guidance, the Hal Roach staff refined Laurel and Hardy's characterizations. Gradually, Stan's persona lost all his aggressiveness, except when provoked. Otherwise, his character was placidly dopey, willingly if ineptly heeding his partner's orders. This dopiness was especially evident in Stan's half-closed eyes. Stan finally realized he did not have to mug in order to garner laughs.

When pleased, he would grin broadly, emanating a childlike serenity. If he got upset, Stan would contort his face into a weeping grimace. His crying expression looked so comically absurd that audiences inevitably laughed. Such was Stan's talent that he could milk humor from tears.

With more experience in front of the camera than Stan, Babe had long mastered the subtleties of film acting. He used his expressive face to demonstrate his self-importance, tempered by an underlying sweetness. It was the sweetness that made Hardy's character so endearing. No matter how much Oliver bossed Stan and no matter how exasperated he was at his partner's bungling, one sensed that Hardy had no ill will toward Laurel.

Babe established a unique rapport with the movie audience. Whenever he was frustrated with his situation, Hardy would mutely address them with an appeal for sympathy. Film historian William K. Everson has pointed out that Oliver did not break character and remove himself from the film's action but invited the audience to share his plight. There was no real self-pity in these looks, just a weary resignation.

Just as Stan and Ollie's characters were further developed in subsequent films, so was their characters' relationship. Although they often annoyed each other and sometimes quarreled, one sensed in the films an underlying devotion to each other. They stuck together no matter how unfortunate circumstances were and the circumstances were always very unfortunate! Their mutual affection imbued the team with a warmth lacking in other comedy duos.

The friendship between Stan and Ollie was a blessing in these movies because often that was all they had. For instance, in *You're Darn Tootin'* Laurel and Hardy lose their jobs, their lodging, and their trousers in that order. As the duo's chronicler Randy Skretvedt states, all they have left is each other. Yet this point was usually humorously presented, without pathos. Moviegoers could freely laugh at Laurel and Hardy's blight without discomfort.

Laurel and Hardy's characters became so likable and believable that they could carry even weak material. The team also benefited from a fine supporting cast. Their most durable foil was James Finlayson, whose talents were better showcased in Laurel and Hardy films than in the solo Stan Laurel films. His mugging perfectly counterpointed Laurel and Hardy's underacting. Another fine foil was a balding, imposing comedian named Edgar Kennedy. Whenever the team annoyed him, he would perform a "slow burn." He would valiantly try to keep his composure but his anger got the better of him and Kennedy would fume, bring his left hand to his head, and slowly drag it downward over his face. This had to been seen to be fully appreciated. Anita Garvin was another worthy supporting player, comically displaying an icy hauteur. She was particularly memorable as a society hostess who hires Laurel and Hardy to serve dinner in *From Soup to Nuts*, struggling to maintain her prestige despite the team's slapstick havoc. A diminutive Englishman named Charlie Hall became known as "The Little Menace" for his expert portrayal of surly characters the duo ran into in various films. That Laurel and Hardy's films were blessed with such gifted supporting players indicate that Roach's studio was an exemplary judge of acting talent.

Laurel and Hardy had hit their stride. But soon they would face a new challenge. Moviemakers had experimented with sound on film since the early twentieth century. Most people dismissed talking pictures as freakish novelties until the fall of 1927 when the Warner Brothers studio released a film with dialogue sequences called *The Jazz Singer*. Audiences thrilled at seeing *and* hearing Broadway musical star Al Jolson in that film. Warner Brothers produced more sound films, known as "talkies", and interest grew. Soon moviegoers considered silent films obsolete.

Like all the other movie studios, the Hal Roach studio decided to convert to sound. Filmgoers would hear Laurel and Hardy for the first time. How would dialogue affect the comedians' characters, carefully crafted in an entirely silent medium?

Photography

Stan Laurel, boss Hal Roach, and Oliver Hardy.

Laurel and Hardy in their first joint appearance on film, *Lucky Dog* (1921).

**In their first official short as a team,
The Second Hundred Years (1927) with Dorothy Coburn.**

In *Sons of the Desert* (1933).

In their Academy Award-winning short
***The Music Box* (1932) with Billy Gilbert.**

In *Babes in Toyland* (1934), battling the dreaded Bogeymen.

In *Way Out West* (1937).

In their last film, *Atoll K* (1951).

Laurel and Hardy Speak!

Stan and Ollie didn't have to worry about sound. Their voices were perfectly suited for their characterizations. Stan's soft, mild voice suited both the gentility and the vacuity of his character. As for Babe, he had a delicate, lilting cadence in his speech, perfect for his character's elegance and pomposity. In the first talkie, Hardy's Southern accent was pronounced. He later modified this accent and thus broadened his appeal to moviegoers in all regions of the United States.

Laurel and Hardy quickly learned how to humorously deliver dialogue. Firstly, they avoided one-liners. Hardy told an interviewer, "The minute you wisecrack, you're fresh. People resent it. Comedy must be believable." Stan realized his character could garner laughs from mangling cliches. For instance, when he tried to deliver the old phrase, "You can lead a horse to water but you can't make him drink", he'd misspeak, "You can lead a horse to water but a pencil must be lead."

What made these gaffes especially hilarious was Stan's innocent delivery, completely unaware that he was spouting nonsense. He also handled his trademark cry effectively. Using a high-pitched squeal, his sobbing routine was even funnier in talkies than it was in silents.

Babe would be given pedestrian remarks and make them funny. Ordinarily, there's nothing humorous about this line, "Here's another nice mess you've gotten me into!"

Delivering this line with comical exasperation to Stan, however, Ollie made this expression hilarious. He made this saying so much his own that it became a catchphrase in Laurel and Hardy's films. Often Ollie would say it at the film's ending as the team found themselves embroiled in yet another calamity.

Laurel and Hardy also maintained their physical comedy. Unlike other comedians who were adjusting to sound, the team did not sacrifice visual slapstick for dialogue. Stan later recalled, "We had decided we weren't talking comedians and of course preferred to do pantomime, like in our silents. So we said as little as possible-only what was necessary to motivate the things we were doing. If there was any plot to be told, we generally would have somebody else tell it...as time went on, we became a little more accustomed, and did more talking than we first intended."

Because the team adjusted so smoothly to sound, their comedies maintained a high standard of quality. By now they were not only popular in the United States but also in Latin America and in Europe. Hal Roach decided that Laurel and Hardy should appear in "foreign" language versions for audiences abroad, speaking in Spanish, French, German, and Italian. Since the comedians only understood English, they learned their "foreign" lines phonetically with the aid of a voice coach.

They would work on four versions of each scene. "It was a long, drawn-out process," Richard Currier recalled. "You'd start in on a scene and it was probably a half hour's worth of rehearsal on each one of 'em with each language coach before the boys got their lines down, so they could say them the way they should sound." The long, hard work paid off handsomely, since their "foreign" language films did well in Latin America and Europe. Even though they were short subjects, they were often run as the main attractions in theatres there.

Back in the United States, Laurel and Hardy began working on films that were longer than two reels. In December 1929 when working on a comedy called *Blotto*, the Roach staff devised so many inspired gags that they decided to expand its running time to thirty minutes. It was released as a three-reeler in February 1930 and in the next two years, the team starred in several more three-reelers. In 1931, they even starred in a four-reeler running forty minutes, *Beau Hunks*. "We made the three and four-reelers because the stories went that far," Roach said.

Laurel and Hardy began appearing in feature films as well. In 1929, Metro Goldwyn-Mayer (MGM), the studio that distributed the Hal Roach comedies, was so impressed with the team's popularity that it used them in a comic sketch in its all-star variety extravaganza, *The Hollywood Revue of 1929*. In 1930, Laurel and Hardy provided comic relief in the filmed opera, *The Rogue Song*. The following year, they completed their first starring feature, *Pardon Us*.

Pardon Us was originally planned as a short called *The Rap.* Because Laurel and Hardy were playing convicts, Roach wanted to use a prison set that had already been constructed for an MGM feature. MGM agreed to let him use the set on the condition that the comedians appear in another feature. Roach wasn't willing, so he built his own prison set. It was so expensive that the only way the film could recoup was to expand it into a feature film.

Pardon Us's scenario, where Stan and Ollie are jailed for selling beer during Prohibition when alcohol was illegal, was slim, with gag sequences like a visit to the dentist only loosely connected to the story. Nevertheless, the comedians' characters were so lovable and vivid that they easily sustained the film's one hour length. *Pardon Us* also showcased the team's musical talents in one scene where Hardy beautifully sang an song dating from the early 1900s, "Lazy Moon," and Stan gracefully performed a soft-shoe dance.

The film was a box office success but Laurel and Hardy did not wish to abandon shorts for features. It was easier to sustain laughs in a short than in a feature. Hal Roach contended, "If you can stop after twenty minutes, you've only got to go up to this peak for your last laugh. But if you've got to go clear to sixty minutes, the last laugh is three times harder. It's that simple. And I don't care how funny a guy is, if you listen to him long enough, you're going to be bored...with him."

Audiences never got bored with Laurel and Hardy. Even when the comedians stopped working on "foreign" language films due to the development of more sophisticated dubbing techniques, they maintained their worldwide popularity. Watching these early

1930s comedies today, one can easily understand why. At least two shorts are now considered classics by fans and scholars.

In *Helpmates*, Ollie holds a wild party when his wife is away. Learning the morning after the bash that Mrs. Hardy is coming home at noon, he begs Stan to help him clean the house. Of course the duo wind up making an even greater mess. At one point, Stan, irked by Ollie's bossiness, declares, "If I had any sense I'd walk out on you."

"Well it's a good thing you haven't any sense!" Ollie shouts.

"It certainly is!" Stan responds.

The humor is enhanced when following this exchange, Stan looks puzzled as he tries to figure out what he has just said.

Miraculously, they manage to tidy the house up. Ollie departs to greet his wife at the train station in his military-looking lodge uniform. (In trying to clean up the house, Stan has ruined all his friend's other clothes.) While Ollie is away, Stan decides to leave a cheery fire in the fireplace. But when he pours gasoline on the logs, he accidentally burns the house down!

Then Hardy returns home with a black eye and without his wife. Instead of saying, "Here's another nice mess you've gotten me into!", Ollie stoically accepts his homelessness, telling his pal, "I'd like to be alone." After Stan leaves, it starts to rain and Hardy gets caught in a downpour. As the film ends, a soaked Ollie sits in his chair resigned to his fate yet determined to maintain his dignity as he flicks a piece of lint from his uniform. This final shot, enhanced by Babe's delicate performance, adroitly mixes humor and pathos.

In early 1932, Laurel and Hardy starred in a three-reeler called

The Music Box. Here, they struggle to carry a player-piano up a long flight of stairs. This effort is hindered by both their own incompetence and some obnoxious people they run into on the way up. One particularly annoying person is the pompous Professor Theodore von Schwartzenhoffen (played by Billy Gilbert) who considers it beneath his dignity to walk around the piano. When they finally reach the top, a postman (Charlie Hall) tells them they could have driven the piano up a road surrounding the stairs. Stan and Ollie backtrack and load the instrument into their horse-drawn wagon so they can proceed up that road.

After they've somehow brought the piano into the house, the owner shows up. He turns out to be the same Professor von Schwartzenhoffen whom Stan and Ollie had antagonized earlier. To make things even worse, the professor *despises* pianos! He proceeds to demolish the instrument with an axe while it plays "The Star Spangled Banner." Then the professor's wife appears, tearfully telling her husband that the piano was supposed be a gift for him. Ostentatiously contrite, von Schwartzenhoffen offers to sign Laurel and Hardy's delivery note. But the pen squirts ink in his face and the film ends with the professor angrily chasing Stan and Ollie out of the house.

The Music Box is a masterpiece of comedy construction. As the characters plod along with their piano delivery, the action never drags. The filmmakers skillfully milk all the humor out of this situation through both clever gags and the comedians' winning personalities. The Academy of Motion Pictures Arts and Sciences, an organization created to honor excellence in films, was so impressed by *The Music Box* that it gave the film the Academy Award ("the Oscar") for Best Short Subject in November 1932.

The film also benefits from Gilbert's hilariously apoplectic performance, enhanced by a comical German accent. Billy Gilbert was a hefty performer who specialized in playing ill-tempered louts and magisterial gentlemen in Laurel and Hardy's films. In the early sound era, the films were still blessed with sterling supporting players. Some of the actors who worked with Stan and Ollie in the silent era like James Finlayson stayed on. Others like Edgar Kennedy left the Roach lot in the early 1930s. They were replaced by other fine performers who worked well with the team. Gilbert was one of them. Mae Busch, who had a humorous sneer and a sharp, ear-piecing voice, excelled at playing nagging wives and unscrupulous schemers.

Even though Leo McCarey had left the Roach lot by the early 1930s, the studio still had fine directors like James W. Horne and James Parrott, who happened to be Charley Chase's brother. They not only understood comedy but respected Laurel's de facto leadership. The films also benefited from lively music scores composed by T. Marvin Hatley and LeRoy Shields. Hatley also provided a theme song that opened every Laurel and Hardy film called "The Dance of the Cuckoos."

Stan and Babe got along well with each other on the set. But they didn't socialize much when they didn't act in front of the camera. While Laurel worked with the directors, editors, and other film crew, Hardy continued to golf and bet at the racetrack. Both were married by the early 1930s. Stan had wed an American actress named Lois Neilson on August 23, 1926. Their daughter, Lois Junior, was born on December 10, 1927. A son, Stanley Robert, was born on May 7, 1930. Sadly, he was two months premature and sickly; he died nine days later. Naturally, this tragedy devastated

Stan but he soon recovered and resumed his work. He adored his daughter but he couldn't spend too much time with her because of his heavy film schedule. Babe remained married to Myrtle. But their marriage was troubled due to Myrtle's drinking problem.

Although Stan now permanently lived in the United States, he never relinquished his British citizenship and remained in touch with his family in his native country, visiting them there in 1927. In 1932, Stan decided to go to Britain again. At that time, Babe was thinking of visiting Canada. He decided instead to go to Britain with Stan when he learned that it had excellent golf courses. So in July of that year, Laurel and Hardy went on a music-hall tour of England and Scotland, hoping to enjoy a nice vacation as well.

But they wouldn't get to relax much. Even before they left Hollywood, MGM was already publicizing the team's trip. The comedians learned on their four-day train journey from Los Angeles to New York City that they couldn't avoid attention. While they changed trains in Chicago, fans, reporters, and photographers surrounded them. MGM arranged a farewell reception for Stan and Babe in New York City. The crowds gathering to watch the team ride down the streets were so large and so fervent that the police had to push the overwhelmed duo into a theater so the mobs wouldn't suffocate them.

The situation in Britain was even more chaotic. They made a personal appearance at a theater called the Empire in Leicester Square in London. As they left the Empire, two thousand fans charged toward them. Since there were only seven policemen, they couldn't control the mob. When Laurel and Hardy managed to get inside the car, fans tore off one of its doors.

At the Central Station in Glasgow, Scotland, six thousand people encircled the comedians and six policemen. Stan almost lost one of his shoes and Ollie nearly collapsed. As they tried to get to the Central Hotel, a stone balustrade guarding one side of the hotel door toppled from the weight of people grabbing it. Consequently two people were crushed by stones, other people fainted, and still others fell into a manhole. Nine people were sent to the hospital.

Laurel and Hardy had little time for sight seeing because they always attracted excited fans. One late night in North Shields, Stan tried to sneak out to see his old home but the crowds caught up with him. After their stay in Britain, Stan and Babe went to Paris, France and experienced the same wild public adulation there.

Finally in September, Laurel and Hardy returned to the United States. They were exhausted from the trip and were astounded by the public reception they had received. More than anything else, this experience overseas made them realize they were now authentic movie stars.

Being movie stars, the film industry considered them too important to work exclusively on shorts. Around the time Laurel and Hardy came back to Hollywood, their second starring feature film, *Pack Up Your Troubles*, was released. In this movie, the comedians are soldiers during World War I. When their friend Eddie is killed in battle, Laurel and Hardy become guardians for his orphaned daughter. For the rest of the film, they try to locate her grandparents so a mean welfare officer won't take her away to an orphanage. The only problem is that her last name is Smith, the most common surname in the United States.

The scenario of *Pack Up Your Troubles*, like that of Laurel and

Hardy's previous starring feature, is weak. The serious elements involving the orphaned girl's plight were already hackneyed in 1932. Fortunately the comedians do well not only in the comedy scenes but in their scenes with the girl, played by Jacquie Lyn. Stan and Babe have a marvelous rapport with her, showering her with fatherly affection without being cloying. The fact that Laurel and Hardy's characters could handle straight scenes demonstrate their essential humanity, an element lacking in other 1930s film comedians' personas. Audiences in 1932 appreciated this quality, making *Pack Up Your Troubles* another box office hit.

During the next few years, Laurel and Hardy alternated between shorts and features. Their next starring feature, released in the spring of 1933, radically differed from their two previous vehicles. This new film, *The Devil's Brother*, was adapted from a century-old comic opera called *Fra Diavolo*. Since it took place in eighteenth century Italy, Stan and Babe abandoned their derbies and suits for period costumes.

The comedians' characters, called Stanlio and Ollio, were not the entire focus of the scenario. Some scenes concentrated on Dennis King, a singer who played a bandit named Fra Diavolo and who sang the film's musical numbers. The comedians' characters were smoothly integrated into a plot involving a robbery as Diavolo's unwilling assistants. King proved an effective straight man for the team, constantly threatening to kill them for bungling and yet so charming and colorful one couldn't dislike him, since he'd never carry out this threat.

The next feature film was *Sons of the Desert*, released at the end of 1933. Fans and scholars today consider it to be one of their best features. This time, Stan and Ollie carried the entire film. The title refers to a lodge that they belong to. The comedians plan to attend a Sons convention in Chicago but Mrs. Hardy (Mae Busch) won't let Ollie go, insisting on taking him to the mountains. So Hardy pretends he's having a nervous breakdown. A doctor, who is in on the ruse, recommends an ocean voyage for him. He forbids Mrs. Hardy to go with him since she is a bad sailor so Ollie insists that Stan should keep him company.

They go to Chicago as planned and enjoy themselves immensely. But when Stan and Ollie arrive home they learn that the ship they were supposed to travel on to Hawaii has sunk! Forced to confront their suspicious wives, the men concoct a wild story in which they managed to reach land by *ship-hiking*. Ollie contends, "Why it's too farfetched *not* to be the truth." Eventually, Mrs. Laurel (Dorothy Christie) coerces Stan into tearfully confessing what actually happened. She rewards his honesty by pampering him like a king. Meanwhile, Mrs. Hardy showers *her* deceitful husband with all the household crockery.

Unlike *Pardon Us* and *Pack Up Your Troubles*, *Sons of the Desert* has a sturdy plot that smoothly flows from one scene to another. There is no dramatic or musical filler to interrupt Laurel and Hardy's shenanigans; the comedians dominate the entire film. Over seventy years after its initial release, *Sons of the Desert* not only ranks as one of the best Laurel and Hardy films, but one of the best film comedies ever.

The team's next feature film appearance was in another all-star extravaganza, *Hollywood Party*, released in 1934. Later that year, they starred in another musical. *Babes in Toyland* was adapted from a Victor Herbert operetta about a land populated by characters from Mother Goose rhymes. As bumbling toymakers named Stannie Dum and Ollie Dee, Laurel and Hardy's childlike personalities are appropriate for the fairy tale land of Toyland.

Stannie misinterprets an order from Santa Claus (Ferdinand Munier) to make six hundred soldiers each one foot high- instead he informs Ollie to make one hundred soldiers each six feet high. This blunder turns out to be a blessing in disguise because the team successfully employs the soldiers to combat the monstrous Bogeymen who threaten to annihilate Toyland. As with the case of *Fra Diavolo*, Laurel and Hardy do not carry the entire film. There are straight musical interludes involving the young romantic leads Little Bo Peep (Charlotte Henry) and Tom Tom the Piper's Son (Felix Knight). But the musical segments are charming and do not detract from Laurel and Hardy's antics.

Babes in Toyland was a box office success when it was released. It remains a holiday staple today, annually televised during the Yuletide season. But Hal Roach did not like the film. His original script, quite different from the one used in the film, was rejected by Stan. Roach believed his original story was much better than the later filmed version written by Stan and other scenarists. This was the beginning of friction between Roach and Laurel over creative control.

The next Laurel and Hardy feature, released in summer of 1935, was a bit of a letdown. In *Bonnie Scotland*, Stan and Ollie accidentally enlist in a regiment in India. Just as accidentally, they suppress a revolt in the film's climax. *Bonnie Scotland* has not aged well. At the time it was made, India was a British colony. This movie glorifies the British domination of this land and depicts anti-British rebels as villains. Thirteen years after the film's release in 1948, Great Britain granted India independence. Now it is difficult for today's audiences to appreciate Stan and Ollie's efforts to uphold British imperialism. Another problem with *Bonnie Scotland* is that once again, Laurel and Hardy alternate scenes with romantic leads. This time, the romantic plot falls flat because it is poorly developed and it has little to do with the team. It doesn't help that the boy, William Janney, is whiny and the girl, June Lang, is vapid.

The Hal Roach staff never had to worry about romantic subplots in Laurel and Hardy's shorts because of their relatively brief running time. Moviegoers didn't care much about scenarios in shorts as long as the gags amused them but they expected features, even comedies, to have sturdy plots to maintain their interest. As lovable and well developed as the team's characters were, the staff wasn't fully confident in utilizing them in feature-length stories. They believed that the team's humor might wear thin if they were the focus of every scene. *Bonnie Scotland* demonstrates that the staff's efforts to rectify this problem were not always successful.

This was a problem that would dog the team for the remainder of the career. After *Bonnie Scotland*'s release, Laurel and Hardy starred in only one more short. Roach, Laurel, and Hardy did not want to give up two-reelers. But the United States was in the middle of the Great Depression which had started with the stock market crash in October of 1929. Now many Americans were impoverished with little money to spend on movies. Movie theater exhibitors felt that shorts were not as important as features and wouldn't attract enough people. So instead of showing filmgoers a features and a short, they began showing two features for the price of one.

Hal Roach realized that in order to survive in the film business, he had to eventually abandon shorts for features. Laurel and Hardy realized that if they were to remain prosperous, they had to do the same. So in August of 1935, their last short, *Thicker Than Water*, was released. Short subjects would survive for over twenty years before television rendered them obsolete. But when Laurel and Hardy abandoned them, they took away much of the market's luster. And the team was deprived of their most ideal medium.

Triumph and Decline

Hal Roach's decision to abandon two-reelers for features affected the Lot of Fun's atmosphere. Because features were more costly than shorts, the cast and crew could less afford to relax and joke on the set. Film schedules were now more regimented because spending time meant spending money. In order to keep Laurel and Hardy's films under budget, Roach asserted stronger financial and artistic control over them.

Roach's greater power further strained his relationship with Stan Laurel. They began to quarrel more frequently over stories. Each man adamantly believed he was the best judge of material for the team. It was Roach's idea to use the team in comic operas and to supply romantic filler in their features. But Stan wanted original scenarios that exclusively focused on the team.

Laurel also was unhappy with his contract. Even though he and Hardy were a team, they had separate contracts. He wanted Roach to give him and Babe a joint contract but the producer wouldn't accept this. If Laurel and Hardy had a joint contract, they could leave Roach together and work for another studio. They couldn't leave together under individual contracts. If Roach wanted to keep Stan in line, he'd threaten to cancel his contract and thus split the team. Neither comedian wished to work solo at this point not only because they cherished their partnership but because it would be financially risky for them to dissolve it.

Roach had the final word on the screenplay for the team's next feature, *The Bohemian Girl*. Like *The Devil's Brother* and *Babes in Toyland*, this film was adopted from an older musical work, in this case an 1843 operetta by Michael Balfe. Released in early 1936, the story was better constructed than *Bonnie Scotland*'s but once again, the team alternated scenes with straight musical numbers.

Roach gave Stan more artistic control for their next film, *Our Relations*. This film was credited as a "Stan Laurel Production." Actually, Stan didn't produce this movie but this credit gave him a semblance of autonomy and it officially confirmed his creative dominance on the set. For the first time since *Sons of the Desert*, Laurel and Hardy would dominate the entire feature.

Indeed, audiences got *two* Laurels and *two* Hardys for the price of *one*. In *Our Relations*, Stan and Ollie play their usual characters who are married and settled down and their long-lost sailor brothers Bert and Alf, unattached and sailing around the world. Throughout the film, other characters mistake Stan and Ollie for Bert and Alf and vice versa. This confusion is complicated when Bert and Alf lose a valuable pearl ring to their twins who are in turned menaced by crooks. The identity mix-up is finally resolved in the end when the twins meet each other.

Our Relations's plot is stronger than the ones for the previous two features. By alternating scenes of Stan and Ollie with Bert and Alf, the comedians effortlessly carry the film without wearing out their welcome. It was a box office success, and not only with ordinary filmgoers. King Edward VIII of Great Britain requested a private screening of the film before it was released there. President Franklin Roosevelt of the United States also enjoyed a private screening just before he made a goodwill tour to Latin America.

The next feature is today considered one of the team's very best. A Western spoof called *Way Out West*, it again focused exclusively on Laurel and Hardy. Before he dies, a friend entrusts them with a deed to a gold mine. They travel to a rough town called Brushwood Gulch to deliver the deed to the friend's daughter. Stan and Ollie have never seen this woman. They accidentally spill the beans about the deed to larcenous saloon owner Mickey Finn (James Finlayson). Finn then has his wife impersonate the daughter. Eventually, the team learns that the real daughter is Finn's servant and they comically struggle to reclaim the deed from him.

Way Out West's scenario breezes along without any lulls. It not only benefits from the judicious use of Laurel and Hardy's characters but also Finlayson's hilarious villainy. The film also showcases the team's musical talents in two numbers- a lovely dance to a sweet song called "At the Ball, That's All" and a charming and funny duet of another song, "The Trail of the Lonesome Pine." In the latter number, Stan's voice suddenly becomes very deep (provided by Chill Wills.) Smacked on the head with a mallet, he finishes the song in a light feminine voice (provided by Rosina Lawrence, who also played the daughter.)

But although their careers were soaring, their personal lives were unhappy. Stan had divorced Lois Neilson in 1933. He commented to a reporter, "When two people reach the place in life where they can no longer share a laugh together, then it is practically impossible to share the same bed and board...We reached the point where we were continually getting on each other's nerves. I'm sure that nothing I did was very amusing to my wife...When we realized that we had reached the point where we could no longer laugh together, then there was nothing else to do...but legally separate."

Hal Roach later recalled, "I think Stan's career was terrifically affected. He was very much in love with Lois and he never dreamed she would really get the divorce. After that, Stan married all those other dames, and it cost him a lot of money."

In 1934, he married Virginia Ruth Rogers. She got along well with his daughter Lois. But by the time he was filming *Way Out West* the marriage had collapsed. Stan told Ruth that he was in love with another woman. But this relationship quickly came to an end.

Hardy divorced his wife Myrtle just before the film was released. Testifying before a court about the strain of dealing with her chronic alcoholism, Oliver burst into tears. The judge ordered the court cleared until Hardy regained his composure. Miraculously, the comedians' ordeals did not affect *Way Out West*. Viewing their lively work in that film, there is no sign of their off-screen troubles.

One would think that after the success of *Our Relations* and *Way Out West,* Hal Roach would produce another pure Laurel and Hardy comedy. Instead, in their next feature *Swiss Miss*, he made the team alternate scenes with another young romantic couple. Like *Bonnie Scotland*, the romantic plot had little to do with Laurel and Hardy's scenario, which in this case made them fumbling mousetrap salesmen in Switzerland forced to slave in a restaurant to pay off an enormous bill. Even worse, the lovers were downright odious. Della Lind as the ingenue was particularly offensive. Hal Erickson points out in a newsgroup called alt.comedy.laurel-hardy that she "callously toys with the moonstruck Ollie's emotions just to prove a point to her equally obnoxious husband." Such behavior makes her completely unlikable.

Stan was unhappy with *Swiss Miss* because he wasn't given enough creative freedom on the set. He devised a sequence where Laurel and Hardy carry a piano across the Alpine gorge. They don't realize that their boss, who is infatuated with the ingenue and wants to get rid of her musician husband, has planted a bomb in the instrument. As they struggle to carry the piano, Stan keeps falling against the keys, threatening to set the bomb off. But without telling Laurel, Roach ordered all references to the bomb removed before *Swiss Miss*'s release. Shots of Stan falling against the keys remained, but they were now pointless.

While making *Swiss Miss*, Stan once again remarried. The new Mrs. Laurel was a Russian singer named Vera Ivanova Shuvalova, known to friends as Illiana. She was tempestuous by nature and she constantly quarreled with Stan. He found refuge at the studio working on the next feature, *Block-Heads*.

Block-Heads was a welcome return to pure comedy, devoid of any romantic subplots. In this film, Stan faithfully guards an army trench in France for twenty years, even after World War I has ended! In the meantime, Ollie, who served with Stan during the war, has settled down to domestic bliss. He is thrilled to learn that his friend has been discovered and immediately rushes to the National Soldiers' Home to see him.

Their reunion sequence demonstrates both the characters' mutual devotion and their trouble communicating with each other. Searching for a chair to read the newspaper, Stan finds a wheelchair with a shortened leg support. To sit comfortably, he tucks his right leg in the support. When Ollie sees him, he thinks that his friend was crippled in combat. When Stan has to give up the wheelchair to its rightful owner, Ollie carries him to the car. It is only when they fall down that Hardy realizes Laurel can still walk.

"Why didn't you tell me you had two legs?" Ollie demands in his uniquely exasperated way.

"Well, you didn't ask me," Stan replies matter-of-factly.

Ollie quickly gets over his irritation and drives his friend to his apartment for a nice meal. But in his unwitting way, Stan proceeds to wreck havoc on his partner's home and marriage.

The story for *Block-Heads* is slight but it smoothly flows without any padding, allowing Laurel and Hardy to engage in delightful slapstick bits that hold the audience's interest. In one inspired segment, they have to walk up a flight of stairs due to a broken elevator. They bump into obnoxious characters, including the ever reliable James Finlayson as a haughty gentleman who challenges Hardy to a fight. Scholars and fans now consider *Block-Heads* to be one of the team's finest features.

But Stan continued to quarrel with Roach behind the set. In the film, Billy Gilbert plays a jealous game hunter who thinks that the pair is fooling with his wife. At the film' end, he shoots at them.

Laurel proposed that the film end with a scene showing their heads in separate trophy mounts over Gilbert's fireplace. Ollie would look at Stan and utter his trademark line, "Well, here's another nice mess you've gotten me into."

The sequence was rather macabre, but it was funny because it came across as cartoonish- after all, Hardy could still talk. Freakish endings had been employed in previous Laurel and Hardy films- in one film, they wind up with their legs twisted around their necks and in another film, somebody turns their heads backwards. But Roach rejected Stan's idea for *Block-Heads*.

Stan could not hide his marital problems. Illiana often publicly embarrassed him with her erratic behavior. Emotionally drained, he suddenly left Los Angeles toward the end of filming. The crew managed to complete the film in his absence. Two weeks later, Stan returned. But Roach was unhappy with both Laurel's unprofessional behavior and the bad publicity his marriage was generating. Stars were expected to project wholesome offscreen reputations for the public. Roach felt that Laurel's marital misadventures were hurting the studio's family-friendly image. On August 12, the Hal Roach studio notified Stan that his contract was terminated.

For a while, it seemed that Laurel and Hardy's partnership was over. Babe bore no ill will toward Stan, but he knew he had to keep working for Roach in order to keep a roof over his head. The studio produced a solo Oliver Hardy feature, *Zenobia*, which was released in 1939. Hardy was delightful in the starring role as a kindly doctor in the post-Civil War South who unties a knot in a carnival barker's elephant and accidentally finds himself the object of the animal's affections. But the film did not do well at the box office. Realizing that Hardy needed Laurel in order to insure profits, Roach rehired Stan in April 1939. By then, Laurel's marriage to Illiana had ended, freeing him of a professional and personal burden. Laurel and Hardy still had separate contracts, but now they were concurrent.

Learning about the team's reunion, a former musical director named Boris Morros wanted to star them in his first film as an independent producer. Laurel and Hardy were receptive and Roach agreed to loan them to Morros for the film. Back in the 1930s, studio moguls who had actors under contract would sometimes loan them to other studios for films. The moguls would be handsomely paid for loaning out their actors.

Morros hired a writer named Alfred Schiller to write an outline for the proposed Laurel and Hardy film. When Stan read the outline, he knew it had to be drastically changed. Schiller was unfamiliar with the work of Laurel and Hardy, depicting them in his scenario as obnoxious jerks who try to outwit each other. Fortunately, Morris gave Laurel creative freedom to revise the script. He even allowed to Stan to bring along other writers from the Roach lot who were experienced with Laurel and Hardy films. Stan would never be granted this autonomy at any other Hollywood studios.

The resulting film, *The Flying Deuces*, was a partial remake of their four-reeler *Beau Hunks*. Like the previous film, this one found Laurel and Hardy fumbling in the French Foreign Legion in the Saharan desert. At the time the film was made, the Legion patrolled much of this area because it was a French colony. While no masterpiece, it was a pleasant film that was true to the team's characters. There was even a musical number where Hardy sang another standard, "Shine On Harvest Moon," while Laurel danced.

Before Laurel and Hardy worked for Morros, they made another film for Hal Roach. It was intended to be a four-reeler and indeed it was released as such in the United States. But while Stan and Ollie were absent from his studio, Roach decided to expand the movie into a feature for the European market. At this point, the team was more highly regarded there than in the United States. When they returned to the Roach lot, the additional footage was shot.

In this new film, *A Chump at Oxford*, Laurel and Hardy accidentally foil a bank robbery. For their reward they want the finest education money can buy. So they find themselves at Oxford University, where the snooty students tease and bully them. When Stan gets hit on the head, he undergoes a radical personality change. He now insists that he is Lord Paddington, an outstanding scholar and athlete.

In assuming this role, Stan winningly plays a character who is the complete opposite of his usual amiable nitwit. Highbrow, self-important and stuffy, he scorns Ollie's humble presence. "Paddington" treats Hardy like a servant rather than an equal, addresses him as "Fatty", and constantly insults him. At one point, he tells Hardy, "Chin up- both of them."

Finally Ollie cannot take this abuse any more and declares he's leaving. But as he's about to go, Stan suffers another blow on the head, returning him to his sweet, simpleminded self. Overjoyed, Ollie embraces his partner. He briefly ponders Stan's remark about his double chin, but quickly laughs it off. The ending is a little abrupt, but it does humorously and touchingly demonstrate Laurel and Hardy's friendship.

Laurel and Hardy then made their last film for Roach, *Saps at Sea*. This time it was released as a feature in both America and abroad, but it was episodic in structure. The movie really consisted of two films in one. The first part concentrates on the team's experiences in an apartment. They discover that the electricity and plumbing have gone haywire. For instance, the radio is covered with frost while the refrigerator plays music. In the meantime, Hardy's nerves are shattered from working at the Sharp and Pierce Horn Manufacturing Company. James Finlayson as a doctor diagnoses Hardy's illness as hornophobia, or a dread of horns.

In the film's second part, the team takes an ocean voyage for Hardy's nerves. A gangster on the lam named Nick (Rychard Cramer) stows away on their boat and the team find themselves in the middle of the sea with him. Stan plays a trombone he brought along, driving Ollie so crazy that he beats the living daylights out of the thug and a coastguard officer. Laurel and Hardy wind up sharing a prison cell with Nick. If *Saps at Sea*'s scenario was weak, at least it focused entirely on the team and there were enough good gags to put the movie over.

While making the film, Hardy proposed to a script clerk named Lucille Jones. He and Stan had first met her on the set of *The Flying Deuces*. Stan was so pleased with her work, that he saw to it that she was hired by the Roach studio to work on the additional *Chump at Oxford* footage and *Saps at Sea*. Babe would offer Lucille a cup of coffee in the mornings and talk with her.

During the production of *Saps at Sea*, Lucille stumbled on a rolled-up carpet and hit her head against one of the cameras. While she was laid up in the hospital, Babe sent a box of roses and a sweet get-well note. Shortly after returning to work, she was typing up some script revisions when Babe approached her.

As he paced the floor, he declared, "I just can't contain myself any longer. I want to tell you the longer I know you the more impressed I am. Don't take this the wrong way, but it would make me the happiest man in the world if you would be my wife."

Lucille accepted his proposal and on March 7, 1940 they got married. This would be a happy marriage that would last until Hardy's death. They would celebrate their wedding anniversary every week at 4:35 PM, the time of the wedding. If Hardy was working on a film, he would wait for the break to telephone Lucille.

Hardy enjoyed Lucille's company so much that he spent all his free time with her. The Hardys had a large backyard where they raised chickens, ducks, turkeys, a cow that had to be returned because she ate the fruit off the trees, and two pigs. The couple intended to kill the pigs for meat but they became attached to Babe, following him around like dogs and nuzzling him. He was so touched by their affection that he couldn't bear to have them slaughtered so the pigs became household pets.

While Hardy was settling down to domestic bliss, he and Laurel thought about their future film career. Their contracts with Roach expired on April 5, 1940. They did not want to renew them because they were determined to become independent producers. They formed their own company, Laurel and Hardy Feature Productions, and searched for a studio that would back their organization and provide them with complete artistic freedom.

The search took months. In the meantime, they toured the country with a new sketch of Stan's called "How to Get a Driver's License." The audiences and critics responded enthusiastically, confirming their popularity. They remained popular abroad as well; soon after the tour ended, they went to Mexico as guests of the country's President Avila Camcho. Surely at least one studio would gladly back Laurel and Hardy films? Finally in April 1941, the team signed up with 20th Century Fox. It was a much bigger studio with larger budgets than Roach's studio. Stan believed this meant he would have a better opportunity to make films his own way.

But he was greatly mistaken. At 20th Century Fox, all employees were compartmentalized. Each person was expected to perform only one assignment. For example, if someone was hired as a cameraman, he was assigned *only* as a cameraman. If someone was hired as a writer, he could do nothing else but write. Fox hired Laurel and Hardy strictly as actors. This meant that neither of them could work in any other department. This was a terrible shock to Stan, who was the creative guiding force behind the team's films at Roach.

The people whom the studio hired for Laurel and Hardy's first Fox film could not grasp the essence of the team's characters. This crew saw Stan and Ollie not as lovable innocents but as irritating dolts. The resulting film, *Great Guns*, is scornful toward their characters. As they blunder in the Army and interfere with the male juvenile's romance, the audience is expected to look down on them rather than sympathize with them. They are saddled with wisecracks that do not suit their genteel characters. For example, in one scene, Ollie is hit by a sack of flour. Stan maliciously laughs at his partner's bad luck and remarks, "You look like a biscuit." Laurel would never have allowed his character to behave like that on the Roach lot.

Despite its mistreatment of the team's characters, *Great Guns* was a box office hit. Television and video players were not available to the public back in 1941 so people could not see earlier and better Laurel and Hardy films like *Sons of the Desert* and *Way Out West*. Only *Great Guns*, which was marketed as a brand new film, was available to them. To audiences, a substandard Laurel and Hardy film was better than none at all.

According to Laurel and Hardy's current contract, they could quit Fox after one film. But although the comedians disliked the studio's controlling atmosphere, they felt they still had to work there because both were burdened with alimony payments and back taxes. So for the next four years, they starred in five more films for Fox. Some of the movies were not so bad but none of them approached the quality of their best work at Roach.

The team's contract with Fox allowed them to work at other studios. Hoping for greater artistic freedom, they starred in two features at MGM. This studio had distributed their Roach films from 1927 to 1938. (United Artists distributed the later Roach films.) But without Roach's influence MGM's environment was distressingly similar to Fox's. The scripts for the MGM films, *Air Raid Wardens* (1943) and *Nothing But Trouble* (1945), attempted to elicit sympathy for the comedians' characters. But the scenarios indulged in misguided pathos that made them pathetic. Part of the appeal of Laurel and Hardy's characters in the Roach films was that even though the odds were against them, they always remained upbeat. It is downright painful to see these formerly endearing optimists wallow in self-pity with such lines like "I guess we're not smart like other people."

Nevertheless, Laurel and Hardy's Fox and MGM films continued to make money. When the team's contract with Fox ended in 1945, the studio offered to renew it. But Laurel and Hardy rejected this offer. They didn't like the idea of grinding out more films without any artistic input. There were no offers from other studios so Laurel and Hardy's Hollywood career ended.

During the years with Fox, Stan's personal life was troubled. He remarried Virginia Ruth Rogers in January 1941 but they soon quarreled and separated, finally divorcing in April 1946. While he was still married to Ruth, he met and fell in love with a widowed blonde Russian opera singer named Ida Kitaeva Raphael. He proposed to her with a big box of twenty-four roses.

But Stan felt he and Ida could not afford a lavish wedding ceremony because he still owed alimony. He told her, "You know, I can't even afford a proper ring, the kind of ring you should have, a wedding ring."

"But we can use my first wedding ring," Ida replied.

Stan said, "Well, if you don't mind."

They planned on a simple and quick ceremony in Yuma, Arizona. Until 1957, nobody had to take a blood test in order to marry there. In May 1946, Stan drove Ida from California to Arizona. But after riding all afternoon, Ida sensed they were in the middle of nowhere due to the smells of cows and barns.

She told Stan, "Wait a minute. Where are we going? I think you've lost your way because I think we've wound up on the range."

She was right. Throughout the rest of the afternoon into the night, he struggled to reach Yuma. By the time he and Ida arrived there, it was early morning on May 6. They had to rouse the justice of the peace out of bed so he could perform the ceremony before hastily rounded up witnesses.

The newly married couple then drove to San Diego, California for their honeymoon. Meanwhile, reporters learned about Stan's latest wedding and soon caught up with him and Ida. Naturally they wanted a statement to the press.

Ida told the reporters, "Please! Please, you boys quote me. Be sure it's accurate: *no more divorces for Stan Laurel!*"

Indeed it was accurate. Stan and Ida remained happily married until his death. In the meantime, theatres in Britain revived older Laurel and Hardy films. They were so popular that Bernard Delfont, a British theatrical impresario, contacted the team late in 1946 and asked them to make a brief tour in that country. Stan was especially delighted with this opportunity. He hadn't been performing since his Fox contract expired and missed the work. The comedians would perform the popular driver's license sketch.

Laurel and Hardy planned to go with their wives to Britain. But just as they were about to leave California, Lucille had to go to the hospital to be treated for a back ailment. This news devastated Babe but Lucille convinced him to honor his contract. She later joined her husband and the Laurels in the midst of the tour.

Stan and Babe arrived in Britain on February 11, 1947. As on their previous tour in 1932, hordes of fans enthusiastically greeted them wherever they went. But the country's atmosphere had changed drastically since the last tour. During World War II in the early 1940s, Britain had been heavily bombed by Germany's Nazi regime. The British government had spent heavily on troops and military equipment to battle the Nazi menace so the people had to make great sacrifices, rationing their food so the soldiers could eat. By the time Stan and Babe arrived in post-war Britain, food was still rationed because the country was struggling to recover from the conflict. Babe would lose ninety pounds on the tour, although he was still hefty. At this point, his normal weight was over three hundred pounds.

Coal was also in short supply resulting in an especially harsh winter. Stan had to postpone a visit to his father Arthur and his sister Olga because they were snowed in inland at Grantham, Lincolnshire. At Newcastle, the theatre where they were to perform lacked heat. The predicament was the same in the hotel. When Stan put the last of the few coal pieces on the fire there, he looked down at it and solemnly declared, "There'll always be an England!"

"There'll Always Be an England" was a popular song that roused the Britishers' patriotism during World War II. Babe and Ida laughed at Laurel's wry use of the phrase. Even when things seemed gloomy, Stan could brighten up everyone's mood with his wit.

Everyone's mood was further brightened by the tour's astounding success. It was originally supposed to last only two weeks, but the British public reaction was so enthusiastic that the company remained in the country for nine months. Then they traveled to Denmark, Sweden, and France. After a brief return to Britain, they

went to France and Belgium. Even though the comedians spoke only English, audiences in all the countries warmly embraced them. They were now middle aged and they hadn't appeared in any recent films but the Europeans still considered them stars. Finally in January 1948, the Laurels and the Hardys returned to the United States.

Back in America, Stan learned he had diabetes. He took a break from work so that, with Ida's help, he could try to regain his health. Babe was offered a character role in a John Wayne film, *The Fighting Kentuckian*. At first, he was reluctant because he feared that taking a solo part would create rumors that he and Laurel were fighting. But Stan assured his partner that while he was recovering Babe could work alone. Hardy distinguished himself as Wayne's friend in *The Fighting Kentuckian*, proving once again he could handle a relatively straight role without resorting to his trademark mannerisms. Hardy also made a cameo in *Riding High*, which was directed by Frank Capra and starred Bing Crosby.

Meanwhile, Laurel and Hardy remained popular in Europe. When World War II raged, audiences there couldn't see any new Laurel and Hardy films. After the war, the last eleven films were finally released there and were well received, particularly in France, Italy, and Britain. In 1950, a conglomerate of French, Italian, and British producers offered the team a new project. The comedians accepted the proposal not only because it was financially rewarding but because it promised them final say on the script. Made in France and generously backed by its government, the film was supposed to be completed in twelve weeks.

It was jinxed from the start. Because this was a multi-national project, a multi-national staff was required. This included two writers from America, one from France, and one from Italy. But the script took three months to complete not only because there was a language barrier but because the writers could not agree on the script. When they finally completed it, they gave it to Stan to evaluate. He pronounced it "rubbish" and revised it with the assistance of an American comedian and gag man named Monty Collins.

When filming began, the same communication difficulties persisted. If anyone debated over how a scene should be played, production would halt and everyone would argue in English, French, and Italian. When they thought the argument had been resolved, they'd start filming again only to find out that the agreement had been lost in the translation.

The director, a Frenchman named Leo Joannon, not only spoke little English but he was very lackadaisical. He spent three days shooting a lake because he thought it looked so beautiful. Joannon's glacial pace annoyed Stan but he could not replace him because of a French union rule that a French production required a French director. Still hoping to restore order, Stan recruited Alfred Goulding, who had directed the team in *A Chump at Oxford*, to manage things. But the French and Italian crew resented Goulding's presence. Eventually, Alf had to leave because of a directing assignment in London, England.

To make things worse, an extreme heat wave affected the comedians' health. Babe's heart began to function erratically and he feared that he wouldn't be able to finish the film. Meanwhile, Stan became ill and drastically lost weight, resulting in hospitalization.

Ida served as his interpreter for the French-speaking hospital staff.

Determined to complete the picture, Stan went back to work when he recovered slightly. But the food served on location made him worse so he could only work for a half an hour at a time. A makeshift hospital was constructed on the set.

Finally, after a year of production, the film was completed in the spring of 1951. The comedians were relieved to return to the United States. The film was released in November 1951 in France and Italy under the title *Atoll K.* It was released in Britain the following year as *Robinson Crusoeland* and in the United States two years later as *Utopia.* Under any title, the film is depressing. It is marred by poor dubbing (the supporting actors did not speak English) and sluggish direction. Even worse is the sight of the two comedians. Stan looks so emaciated and forlorn one fears he may keel over at any minute while Hardy is so grotesquely obese that his figure no longer generates a jolly sense of fun but a serious health concern. Sadly, *Atoll K* would be the team's last picture.

But Laurel and Hardy were not forgotten. A new entertainment medium called television would revive the team's popularity. A TV distributor called Regal Films obtained the rights to Stan and Ollie's classic Hal Roach films. Youngsters who weren't born when the films were first released were introduced to them on television. They responded eagerly to the films, proving the team's timelessness.

The Final Years

By the end of 1951, Stan was healthy enough to work. A Japanese film studio and an Italian film company had made tentative offers to the team but neither of them materialized. Laurel and Hardy decided instead to tour Britain and Northern Ireland. Stan composed a sketch for this tour called "A Spot of Trouble" based on one of their sound Roach two-reelers, *Night Owls.* In this skit, a policeman convinces the comedians to rob a house so that he can nab them to impress his chief. He assures Stan and Ollie they'll get off easy. Naturally, the boys bungle the job. "A Spot of Trouble" was a big hit, playing in theatres from February to September 1952. The comedians also endeared themselves to the British by personally greeting them in the theatre and signing autographs. Despite their exhaustion from the hectic touring, Laurel and Hardy always took time to meet with their fans.

In September 1953, the team toured Britain and Northern Ireland again. It was less than a year since their last tour. According to immigration laws, Hardy had to wait a full year before setting foot in Great Britain because he was an American citizen. Until then, Hardy could only work in Northern Ireland, which was and still is part of the British kingdom. He had to enter Northern Ireland from the Republic of Ireland.

So on September 9, 1953, the team arrived at the small port of Cobh in southern Ireland to rehearse. There was no advance publicity but everybody in the town knew that Stan and Ollie were coming. The people crowded the dock, waving and shouting their welcome, and all the ships and boats in the harbor blew their whistles and sounded their horns. While the crowds rushed to see and greet Laurel and Hardy, the cathedral's bells tolled their theme song, "The Dance of the Cuckoos." The sound of the bells moved Stan and Babe to tears.

For this tour, Stan wrote a new sketch, "Birds of a Feather." In this sketch, Laurel and Hardy get jobs as whiskey tasters. "The more we drink, the more we earn," Stan suggests. They get so drunk that Ollie tries to fly like a bird and Stan believes his partner can do it. Both wind up in a sanitarium as guinea pigs for a crazy doctor's experiment.

Once again, British audiences enthusiastically responded to the team's antics. But Hardy's health was declining since his weight was now over 350 pounds. On May 17, 1954, Hardy was troubled by an infection before performing with Laurel at a theatre in Plymouth, England. The following day, Babe was too sick to work. Doctors discovered that he had suffered a mild heart attack, bringing the tour to an abrupt end. Stan sadly told the local press, "I am completely lost without Hardy. We do comedy sketches- situations. I am not a gag man."

So Laurel and Hardy sailed back to the United States. They would never tour again. But despite Babe's condition the team still dreamed of future work projects. On December 1, 1954, they were guests on the television show *This is Your Life*. Each episode of this show celebrated the life and times of a celebrity. Host Ralph Edwards arranged for family and friends to appear on the show to surprise and celebrate the guest of honor.

Although Stan performed graciously on the show, he wasn't pleased with it. A perfectionist, he hated to appear in front of an audience unprepared. But he remained enthusiastic about the medium of television. He even contemplated starring with his partner in a series of one-hour TV specials based on fairy tales called *Laurel and Hardy's Fabulous Fables*. But this idea would never materialize.

In June 1955, Stan suffered a stroke leaving him temporarily paralyzed on his left side. Meanwhile, Babe continued to have heart trouble and suffered a gall bladder attack. He decided to go on a crash diet and eventually lost 150 pounds. His appearance changed so drastically that he no longer resembled the portly icon who had graced the comedies. The physical contrast between Stan and Ollie hardly existed anymore.

The public got the chance to see the newly trim Hardy when he and Laurel posed for a press photo shoot in the summer of 1956. By this time, Stan was recovering nicely from the stroke. But the team's friends were aghast at Babe's altered appearance. Hardy was so devastated by their reaction that he went into seclusion, seeing no one except Lucille, Stan, Ida, and a few close friends. Then on September 14, he suffered a massive stroke that left him mute and paralyzed.

Babe would never recover. His brain was also affected. Even reading a newspaper and watching television was difficult because he could not focus on these tasks. Despite his inability to speak, Lucille could sense his frustration. She later recalled, "Sometimes he got so upset over his inability to get better that it seemed he almost wished it was all over with." Whenever Babe was relatively lucid, Lucille would call Stan and he would come to visit his former partner. Hardy struggled to communicate with Laurel using his eyes and fingers. Stan was deeply saddened by his old friend's condition, which was further worsened by cancer.

Finally, after suffering two more strokes, Hardy died on August 7, 1957 at the age of sixty-five. "It was a blessing for Oliver. He is finally out of his suffering," Lucille told the press. Stan was greatly affected by Hardy's passing. He could not attend the funeral because he was ill at the time. Talking to the press, he said, "What is there to say? He was like a brother to me. This is the end of the history of Laurel and Hardy."

For Stan, Hardy's death also meant the end of his show business career. Alimony payments had depleted much of his wealth, but he was financially comfortable and could afford to take it easy. He told a friend, "They say I'm not a millionaire any more, They're crazy, I've got Ida."

Even though Stan was retired, he was not forgotten. He was still deluged by fan mail. Stan always answered every letter, even though he received so many he was always months behind. Unlike other celebrities, he let his address remain in the public telephone books so anyone could phone or visit him. Stan even allowed one fan named Mike Polacek to stay at his house for five days. Although he wasn't a celebrity, the Laurels treated him, in Polacek's words, "like a king," even allowing him to take home movies.

In 1961, the Academy of Motion Picture Arts and Sciences awarded Stan an Oscar "for creative pioneering in the field of cinema comedy." Laurel could not personally attend the ceremony because of illness. Danny Kaye, a younger and active comedian whom Stan admired, accepted the award for him and it was delivered to Laurel's house. He was thrilled but he missed Babe and wished he was still alive to share his glory.

The team's films continued to be shown on television but Stan didn't like watching them. He felt that commercial interruptions disrupted the films' flow and continuity. Stan complained, "Why see a lot of good hard work turned into a jigsaw puzzle? I'd even be willing to edit them for nothing but I know they don't care."

But Stan enjoyed creating Laurel and Hardy gags for fun. He knew they would never be used, but devising them was a creative way of coping with his partner's death. As for his own health, it was generally stable despite his diabetes and eye problems. Then on February 23, 1965, Stan suddenly died of a heart attack at the age of seventy-four. He kept his sense of humor to the very end, his last exchange with his nurse in the form of a joke.

Before Stan died, he gave his blessing to a group of fans who wished to form an official Laurel and Hardy fan club. Called the Sons of the Desert, after one of the team's best films, it established its headquarters in New York, NY. Soon branches of the Sons of the Desert, known as "tents," were set up all over the country. The tents named themselves after other Laurel and Hardy films such as the Way Out West tent in Los Angeles, California and the Two Tars tent in Philadelphia, Pennsylvania.

Today, there are almost 220 tents all over the world, demonstrating the team's timeless and worldwide appeal. At each of these tents, fans gather to discuss their appreciation of the comedians and to enjoy their films. Every year, there is an international convention where fans from tents all over the world get together to celebrate the memory of Laurel and Hardy.

For many years, Laurel and Hardy's films were shown regularly on television. People who weren't even born when the comedians passed on have become lifelong fans through viewing the team's antics on the small screen. Regrettably, these films seldom show up on TV anymore. Because they are in black and white and were made over fifty years ago, most television stations do not consider them commercial. It is a shame that the television industry generally ignores any entertainment that is not "new." Fortunately, some of their films are now available on DVD for rental and for purchase. As long as the Sons of the Desert continue to honor the team and as long as their films continue to be available, Stan Laurel and Oliver Hardy will always be remembered and beloved.

Why are Laurel and Hardy still remembered and beloved? We still laugh at them as much as audiences did when their films were first released. But if the team was merely funny, they wouldn't be cherished today. Laurel and Hardy's greatest appeal is their friendliness. We regard them not only as entertaining buffoons but as welcome companions. As much as we are amused by their incompetence, we are touched by their sweetness and mutual devotion. Because we love their characters, we never tire of them. It is their essential humanity that makes Laurel and Hardy great.

Laurel and Hardy's Joint Filmography

Films are listed in the order of their release rather than in the order of production. For example, in 1927, Hal Roach stopped producing shorts for Pathe' Exchange and started producing them for M-G-M. Some completed Pathe' Exchange shorts were released after some of the first M-G-M shorts. Also, when the Roach studio converted to sound, the first few talkies were released before a few already completed silents.

Silent Shorts Before They Were Officially Teamed

(All are two-reelers. With the exception of the first short, all are produced by Hal Roach.)

Lucky Dog- Produced by G.M. Anderson- Released December 1921 by Metro.

45 Minutes from Hollywood- Released December 26, 1926 by Pathe' Exchange.

Duck Soup- Released March 13, 1927 by Pathe' Exchange.

Slipping Wives- Released April 3, 1927 by Pathe' Exchange.

Love 'Em and Weep- Released June 12, 1927 by Pathe' Exchange.

Why Girls Love Sailors- Released July 17, 1927 by Pathe' Exchange.

With Loves and Hisses- Released August 18, 1927 by Pathe' Exchange.

Sugar Daddies- Released September 10, 1927 by M-G-M.

Sailors, Beware!- Released September 27, 1927 by Pathe' Exchange.

Now I'll Tell One- Released October 5, 1927 by Pathe' Exchange.

Do Detectives Think?- Released November 20, 1927 by Pathe' Exchange.

Flying Elephants- Released January 28, 1928 by Pathe' Exchange.

Starring Silent Shorts After Laurel and Hardy Were Officially Teamed
(All of them are produced by Hal Roach and released by M-G-M.)

The Second Hundred Years- Released October 8, 1927.

Call of the Cuckoos- Released October 15, 1927.

Hats Off- Released November 5, 1927.

Putting Pants on Philip- Released December 3, 1927.

The Battle of the Century- Released December 31, 1927.

Leave 'Em Laughing- Released January 28, 1928.

The Finishing Touch- Released February 25, 1928.

From Soup to Nuts- Released March 24, 1928.

You're Darn Tootin'- Released April 21, 1928.

Their Purple Moment- Released May 19, 1928.

Should Married Men Go Home?- Released September 8, 1928.

Early to Bed- Released October 6, 1928.

Two Tars- Released November 3, 1928.

Habeas Corpus- Released December 1, 1928.

We Faw Down- Released December 29, 1928.

Liberty- Released January 26, 1929.

Wrong Again- Released February 23, 1929.

That's My Wife- Released March 23, 1929.

Big Business- Released April 20, 1929.

Double Whoopee- Released May 18, 1929.

Bacon Grabbers- Released October 19,1929.

Angora Love- Released December 14, 1929.

Starring Sound Shorts

(All are two-reelers produced by Hal Roach and released by M-G-M unless noted otherwise.)

Unaccustomed As We Are- Released May 4, 1929.

Berth Marks- Released June 1, 1929.

Men O'War- Released June 29, 1929.

Perfect Day- Released August 10, 1929.

They Go Boom- Released September 21, 1929.

The Hoose-Gow- Released November 16, 1929.

Night Owls- Released January 4, 1930.

Blotto-Three Reels- Released February 8, 1930.

Brats- Released March 22, 1930.

Below Zero- Released April 26, 1930.

Hog Wild- Released May 31, 1930.

The Laurel-Hardy Murder Case- Three Reels- Released September 6, 1930.

Another Fine Mess- Three Reels- Released November 29, 1930.

Be Big- Three Reels- Released February 7, 1931.

Chickens Come Home- Three Reels- Released February 21, 1931.

Laughing Gravy- Released April 4, 1931.

Our Wife- Released May 16, 1931.

Come Clean- Released September 19, 1931.

One Good Turn- Released October 31, 1931.

Beau Hunks- Four Reels- Released December 12, 1931.

Helpmates- Released January 23, 1932.

Any Old Port- Released March 5, 1932.

The Music Box- Three Reels- Released April 16, 1932.

The Chimp- Three Reels- Released May 21, 1932.

County Hospital- Released June 25, 1932.

Scram!- Released September 10, 1932.

Their First Mistake- Released November 5, 1932.

Towed in a Hole- Released December 31, 1932.

Twice Two- Released February 25, 1933.

Me and My Pal- Released April 22, 1933.

The Midnight Patrol- Released August 3, 1933.

Busy Bodies- Released October 7, 1933.

Dirty Work- Released October 28, 1933.

Oliver the Eighth- Released January 13, 1934.

Going Bye-Bye!- Released June 23, 1934.

Them Thar Hills- Released July 21, 1934.

The Live Ghost- Released December 8, 1934.

Tit for Tat- Released January 5, 1935.

The Fixer-Uppers- Released February 9, 1935.

Thicker Than Water- Released March 16, 1935.

Starring Features

Pardon Us- Produced by Hal Roach- Released August 15, 1931 by M-G-M.

Pack Up Your Troubles- Produced by Hal Roach- Released September 17, 1932 by M-G-M.

Fra Diavolo (a.k.a *The Devil's Brother*)- Produced by Hal Roach- Released May 5, 1933 by M-G-M.

Sons of the Desert- Produced by Hal Roach- Released December 29, 1933 by M-G-M.

Babes in Toyland- Produced by Hal Roach- Released November 30, 1934 by M-G-M.

Bonnie Scotland- Produced by Hal Roach- Released August 23, 1935 by M-G-M.

The Bohemian Girl- Produced by Hal Roach- Released February 14, 1936 by M-G-M.

Our Relations- Produced by Stan Laurel for Hal Roach- Released October 30, 1936 by M-G-M.

Way Out West- Produced by Stan Laurel for Hal Roach- Released April 16, 1937 by M-G-M.

Swiss Miss- Produced by Hal Roach- Released May 20, 1938 by M-G-M.

Block-Heads- Produced by Hal Roach- Released August 19, 1938 by M-G-M.

Flying Deuces- Produced by Boris Morros- Released October 20, 1939 by RKO-Radio Pictures.

A Chump at Oxford- Produced by Hal Roach- Released February 16, 1940 by United Artists.

Saps at Sea- Produced by Hal Roach- Released May 30, 1940 by United Artists.

Great Guns- Released October 10, 1941 by Twentieth Century Fox.

A-Haunting We Will Go- Released August 7, 1942 by Twentieth Century-Fox.

Air Raid Wardens- Released April 4, 1943 by M-G-M.

Jitterbugs- Released June 11, 1943 by Twentieth-Century Fox.

The Dancing Masters- Released November 19, 1943 by Twentieth-Century Fox.

The Big Noise- Released September 1944 by Twentieth-Century Fox.

Nothing But Trouble- Released March 1945 by MGM.

The Bullfighters- Released May 18, 1945 by Twentieth-Century Fox.

Atoll K (a.k.a *Utopia* a.k.a *Robinson Crusoeland*) Italian coproduction by Les Films Sirius (France), Franco-London Films S.A. (France) and Fortezza Film (Italy)- Released November 21, 1951.

Supporting Appearances and Cameos In Shorts And Features
(All are sound except when noted.)

Call of the Cuckoos- Two Reels- Silent. Produced by Hal Roach. Released October 15, 1927 by M-G-M. The team make a cameo in this comedy starring Max Davidson.

The Hollywood Review of 1929- Feature- Released November 23, 1929 by MGM. Laurel and Hardy are among the players in this star-studded variety extravaganza.

The Rogue Song- Feature- Released May 10, 1930 by M-G-M. Laurel and Hardy provide comic relief in this opera film starring singer Lawrence Tibbett.

The Stolen Jools- Two Reels- Released April 1931 by Paramount and National Screen Service. Laurel and Hardy make a cameo in a star-studded short made to raise funds for the relief work of the National Variety Artists' tuberculosis sanitarium.

On the Loose- Two Reels- Produced by Hal Roach. Released December 26, 1931 by M-G-M. The team make a cameo in this comedy starring Thelma Todd and Zasu Pitts.

Wild Poses- Two Reels- Produced by Hal Roach. Released October 28, 1933 by M-G-M. The team make a cameo in this comedy starring the children's troupe called "Our Gang" (later known as "The Little Rascals" on television.)

Hollywood Party- Feature- Released June 1, 1934 by M-G-M. Laurel and Hardy are among the featured players in another star-studded variety extravaganza.

On the Wrong Trek- Two Reels- Produced by Hal Roach. Released April 16, 1936 by M-G-M. The comedy team make a cameo in this comedy starring Charley Chase.

Pick a Star- Feature- Released May 21, 1937 by M-G-M. Laurel and Hardy perform two routines in this musical starring Jack Haley and Patsy Kelly.

The Tree in a Test Tube- One Reel- Produced by the U.S. Department of Agriculture, Forest Service–Released 1943. The team does a comedy routine in this short made by the U.S. government to support the World War II effort.

Stan Laurel's Solo Filmography

1917
Nuts in May (Stanley Comedies/Bernstein Productions)

Universal, Nestor, and L-Ko
1918
Phoney Photos, Hickory Hiram, Whose Zoo, O It's Great to Be Crazy

Rolin-Hal Roach
1918
Do You Love Your Wife, Just Rambling Along, Hoot Mon, No Place Like Jail, Hustling for Health

Vitagraph Pictures
1918
Huns and Hyphens, Bears and Bad Men, Frauds and Frenzies

Amalgamated Producing (G.M. Anderson)
1922
A Weak-End Party, The Handy Man, The Egg, The Pest, Mixed Nuts (released 1925), *Mud and Sand*

1923
When Knights Were Cold

Hal Roach–Pathe'
1923
Under Two Jags, The Noon Whistle, White Wings, Pick and Shovel, Kill or Cure, Collars and Cuffs, Gas and Air, Oranges and Lemons, Short Orders, Save the Ship, A Man About Town, Roughest Africa, Scorching Sands, The Whole Truth, Frozen Hearts, The Soilers, Mother's Joy

1924
Smithy, Zeb vs. Paprika, Postage Due, Brothers Under the Chin, Wide Open Spaces, Rupert of Hee Haw, Short Kilts

Joe Rock
1924
Detained, Mandarin Mix-Up, Monsieur Don't Care, West of Hot Dog

1925
Somewhere in Wrong, Twin, Pie-Eyed, The Snow-Hawk, Navy Blue Days, The Sleuth, Dr. Pyckle and Mr. Pryde, Half a Man

Hal Roach–Pathe'
1925
As director: *Chasing the Chaser, Unfriendly Enemies, Yes, Yes, Nanette, Moonlight and Noses*

1926
As director: *Wandering Papas, Wise Guys Prefer Brunettes, Get 'Em Young* (co-director, co-writer, actor); as writer: *Starvation Blues, Don Key (Son of Burro), Your Husband's Past, What's the World Coming To* (also acted), *Dizzy Daddies, Wife Tamers, Madame Mystery* (co-directed), *Never Too Old* (co-

directed), *The Merry Widower* (co-directed), *Raggedy Rose* (co-wrote, co-directed), *Along Came Auntie, Should Husbands Pay* (co-directed), *Galloping Ghosts* (released 1928); as co-writer: *The Nickel Hopper, On the Front Page* (also acted)

1927

As actor: *Seeing the World, Eve's Love Letters*

1928

As actor: *Should Tall Men Marry*

Oliver Hardy's Solo Filmography

Lubin Company
1914

Outwitting Dad, Casey's Birthday, Building a Fire, He Won a Ranch, For Two Pins, The Particular Cowboys, A Tango Tragedy, A Brewerytown Romance, The Female Cop, Good Cider, Long May it Wave, His Sudden Recovery, Who's Boss, The Kidnapped Bride, Worms Will Turn, The Rise of the Johnsons, He Wanted Work, They Bought a Boat, Back to the Farm, Making Auntie Welcome, The Green Alarm, Never Too Old, A Fool There Was, Pins Are Lucky, Jealous James, When the Ham Turned, The Smuggler's Daughter, She Married for Love, The Soubrette and the Simp, The Honor of the Force, Kidnapping the Kid, She Was the Other, The Daddy of Them All, Mother's Baby Boy, The Servant Girl's Legacy, He Wants His Pants, Dobs at the Shore, The Fresh Air Cure, Weary Willie's Rags

1915

What He Forgot, They Looked Alike, Spaghetti and Lottery, Gus and the Anarchists, Cupid's Target, Shoddy the Tailor, The Prize Baby, An Expensive Visit, Cleaning Time, Mixed Flats, Safety Worst, The Twin Sister, Who Stole the Doggies?, A Lucky Strike, Matilda's Legacy, Capturing Bad Bill, Her Choice, Cannibal King, What a Cinch, The Dead Letter, Avenging Bill, The Haunted Hat, Babe's School Days, Edison Bugg's Invention, A Terrible Tragedy, It Happened in Pikersville

Edison Company
It May Be You, Not Much Force, Poor Baby, Clothes Make the Man, The Simp and the Sophomores

Wharton Films (Ithaca, New York)
The Bungalow Bungle, Three Rings and a Goat, A Rheumatic Joint, The Lilac Splash

Miscellaneous New York Films
Ethel's Romeos (Casino Star/Gaumont), *Fatty's Fatal Fun* (Starlight/Pathe'), *Something in Her Eye* (Novelty/Mutual), *A Janitor's Joyful Job* (Novelty/Mutual), *The Crazy Clock* (Wizard/World Film Corp.)

Vim Comedies
1915
The Midnight Prowlers, Pressing Business, Love, Pepper and Sweets, Strangled Harmony, Speed Kings, Mixed and Fixed, Ups and Downs

1916
This Way Out, Chickens, Frenzied Finance, A Special Delivery, Busted Hearts, A Sticky Affair, Bungles' Rainy Day, One Too Many, Bungles Enforces the Law, The Serenade, Bungles' Elopement, Nerve and Gasoline, Bungles Lands a Job, Their Vacation, Mamma's Boys, The Battle Royal, All for a Girl, Hired and Fired, What's Sauce for the Goose, The Brave Ones, The Water Cure, Thirty Days, Baby Doll, The Schemers, Sea Dogs, Hungry Hearts, Never Again, Better Halves, A Day at School, Spaghetti, Aunt Bill, The Heroes, Human Hounds, Dreamy Knights, Life Savers, Their Honeymoon, The Tryout, Royal Blood, The Candy Trail, The Precious Parcel, A Maid to Order, Twin Flats, A Warm Reception, Pipe Dreams, Mother's Child, Prize Winners, The Guilty Ones, He Winked and Won, Fat and Fickle (last three directed by Oliver Hardy)

1917
The Boycotted Baby, The Other Girl, The Love Bugs, A Mix Up in Hearts, Wanted a Bad Man (all four directed by Oliver Hardy)

King Bee
1917

In Jacksonville, Florida: *Back Stage, The Hero, Dough-Nuts, Cupid's Rival, The Villain;* in New York and New Jersey: *The Millionaire, The Goat, The Fly-Cop, The Chief Cook, The Candy Kid, The Hobo, The Pest, The Band Master;* in Hollywood, California: *The Slave*

1918

In Hollywood, California: *The Stranger, His Day Out, The Rogue, The Orderly, The Scholar, The Messenger, The Handy Man, Bright and Early, The Straight and Narrow, Playmates, Beauties in Distress, He's In Again, Married to Order*

L-Ko Studios
1918

Business Before Honesty, Hello Trouble, Painless Love, The King of the Kitchen, Distilled Love (released 1920)

1919

The Freckled Fish, Hop the Bellhop, Lions and Ladies, Hearts in Hock

Vitagraph Pictures
1919

Soapsuds and Sapheads, Jazz and Jailbirds, Mules and Mortgages, Tootsies and Tamales, Healthy and Happy, Flips and Flops, Yaps and Yokels, Dull Care, Mates and Models, Squabs and Squabbles, The Head Waiter, Switches and Sweeties, Bungs and Bunglers, Dames and Dentists, Maids and Muslin

1920

Squeaks and Squawks, Fists and Fodder, Pals and Pugs, He Laughs Last, Springtime, The Decorator, The Stage Hand, The Backyard, His Jonah Day, The Trouble Hunter

1921

The Nuisance, The Mysterious Strangler, The Blizzard, The Tourist, The Rent Collector, The Bakery, The Fall Guy, The Bellhop, The Sawmill

1922

The Show, A Pair of Kings, Fortune's Mask, The Little Wildcat, Golf, The Agent, The Counter Jumper

1923

No Wedding Bells, The Barnyard, The Midnight Cabaret, The Gown Shop, Lightning Love, Horseshoes

1924

Trouble Brewing, The Girl in the Limousine, Her Boy Friend, Kid Speed

1925

The Wizard of Oz

Arrow Pictures
1925

Stick Around, Rivals, Hey Taxi, Hop To It, They All Fall, Fiddlin' Around, The Joke's On You

Hal Roach-Pathe'
1925

Wild Papa, Neptune's Stepdaughter, Isn't Life Terrible, Should Sailors Marry, Yes, Yes, Nanette, Wandering Papas

Independent Larry Semon Films

The Perfect Clown, Stop, Look, Listen (released 1926)

Fox
1925
The Gentle Cyclone

1926
A Bankrupt Honeymoon

Hal Roach-Pathe'
1926
Madame Mystery, Say It with Babies, Long Fliv the King, Thundering Fleas, Along Came Auntie, Two Time Mama, Bromo and Juliet, Crazy Like a Fox, Galloping Ghosts (released 1928), *Be Your Age, The Nickel Hopper*

1927
Mack Sennett
Crazy to Act

Hal Roach-Pathe'
Why Girls Say No, Honorable Mr. Buggs, Should Men Walk Home?, No Man's Law, Fluttering Hearts, Baby Brother

Hal Roach-MGM
1927
Love 'Em and Feed 'Em

1928
Barnum and Ringling, Inc.

As co-writer

Quicksands (Howard Hawks, 1923)

Later Solo Films After The Teaming

Zenobia (Hal Roach-United Artists, 1939)

The Fighting Kentuckian (Republic, 1949)

Riding High (Columbia, 1950)

Bibliography

Books

Gehrig, Wes D. *Laurel and Hardy: A Bio-Bibliography*. New York, NY: Greenwood Press, 1990.

Guiles, Fred Lawrence. *Stan: The Life of Stan Laurel*. New York, NY: Stein and Day, 1980.

Louvish, Simon. *Stan and Ollie: The Roots of Comedy*. New York, NY: Thomas Dunne Books, 2002.

McCabe, John. *Babe: The Life of Oliver Hardy*. Secaucus, NJ: Carol Pub. Group, 1989.

McCabe, John. *The Comedy World of Stan Laurel*. Beverly Hills, CA: Moonstone Press, 1990.

McCabe, John. *Mr. Laurel and Mr. Hardy*. New York, NY: New American Library, 1985.

Owen-Pawson, Jenny and Bill Mouland. *Laurel Before Hardy*. Westmoreland Gazette, Kendall, 1984.

Skretvedt, Randy. *Laurel and Hardy: The Magic Behind the Movies*. Beverly Hills, CA: Past Times Publishing, 1996.

Stone, Rob, with David Wyatt. *Laurel or Hardy: The Solo Films of Stan Laurel and Oliver "Babe" Hardy*. Temecula, CA: Split Reel, 1996.

Websites

Leave 'em Laughing at www.angelfire.com/comics/lh/

Newsgroups

alt.comedy.laurel-hardy